MIRACLE CURE?

F.D.A. DISCLAIMER:

The information in this book is for information and research only, and is not intended to diagnosis, treat, cure, or prevent any disease. These statements have not been evaluated by the F.D.A. Please consult your family physician before using any information in this book.

TABLE OF CONTENTS

"It is not the germs we need worry about. It is our inner terrain." ~ Louis Pasteur

"It is clear to me how this way of eating can totally change your life. It's a revelation, a way of looking at the world in a new light. It affects the way we look at ourselves, and disease, and how the food we put into our bodies affects everything we do."

~ **Jane Clayson,** *CBS News*

"Tired? Bloated? Can't Lose Weight? A pH imbalance may be to blame! Lose 25 lbs. in 4 weeks on the revolutionary new pH Miracle Diet! Breakthrough research shows that the acidity of common foods is making us sick, tired, and very fat. Restoring ideal health and reaching an ideal weight is as easy as building your meals around foods that neutralize acid."

~ *Woman's World Magazine*

"A diet that focuses on weight-loss, fats, or calories will not necessarily lead to better health or even a slimmer body. Instead, you must focus on how acidic your body is. The resulting diet change will inevitably lead to better weight control, and more importantly, disease-free life. There is only one disease — The constant over-acidification of the body."

~ **Dr. Robert O. Young**

This final quote is where I got the title for this book. So with all this said, please turn the page and begin…

This Book Can Save Your Life Make You Set for Life!

Thank you for purchasing this book and reading it. As the headline above says, this really does have the power to SAVE YOUR LIFE! That's a mighty bold statement — so let me address it first. **This book will tell you about what I believe is a powerful 'cure' for what some leading experts say is the '#1 CAUSE of every disease.'**

Yes, many people say that EXCESS BODY ACIDITY (E.B.A.) is the 'Silent Killer' that may be slowly killing you right now. This book will tell you WHY we believe this is true and about THE SIMPLE REMEDY that can combat this terrible problem. I believe that you CARE DEEPLY about your health or you wouldn't have bought this book or be reading my words.

Is this true? IF SO — then what you're about to read will be nothing short of...

SHOCKING!!!

Yes, I believe that you will be absolutely shocked when you discover what people are saying about the danger of E.B.A. and what it may be doing to your body right now. **And the more you read the in-depth research I am about to reveal to you, I am convinced that you will say to yourself...**

"This really is a MIRACLE CURE!"

Of course, that's only my belief and opinion. You could go through this book and still have STRONG DOUBTS about all of this and that's perfectly okay. After all, there is so much health information out there and sometimes none of us knows exactly what is true and not.

So it's okay to be a little bit skeptical about this information. After all, as you're about to see, some of our research makes some VERY BOLD STATEMENTS and really is shocking! **So keep an open mind and think carefully about everything you're about to read.** If even part of this is true, this really can save your life. And it's not every day that you can buy a book that helps you live longer, feel better, have more energy, and safeguard yourself against a wide variety of diseases that cause others to SUFFER

GREATLY and die before their time. And yet, **I firmly believe that this research on the dangers of E.B.A. (that could be building up in your body right now) and how to COMBAT this terrible problem can add years to your life and life to your years.** Now, before I move on, I must give you a powerful and clear...

WARNING!!!

HERE IT IS: The only people I know of who could ever promise a genuine 'MIRACLE CURE' for any disease, let alone 'every' disease, is the American Medical Association (the A.M.A.) and the Food and Drug Administration (the F.D.A.). There may be some other official Government organizations that could promise a genuine 'MIRACLE CURE' that I don't know about. So, that's why all of my business and legal advisors persuaded me to put the "?" in the title. Please make a note of this important distinction.

This is very important, before we go on.

You see, as the legal disclaimer in the beginning of this book states: "We are not doctors or even nutrition experts. **All of the information in SECTION ONE and TWO of this book was compiled from our research, which was done mostly on the Internet and represents the collective 'voice' of other leading experts, not us."** This legal notice is VERY IMPORTANT because I have a healthy respect (fear?) of the United States Government and do not want to do anything to upset the government agents and agencies that monitor the health and nutrition industry.

Again, the only people or agencies that I know of who can make a legitimate claim that they have discovered a 'MIRACLE CURE' for any or every disease is the A.M.A. and/or the F.D.A. and I am NOT affiliated with either one of those agencies. Do you understand this? GOOD!!! I hope so because the last thing you and I would ever want is for the government to come knocking on our door with a book that we had published in their hands!

I have a healthy respect for the government watchdogs that regulate the health industry. Plus, I grew up in the law enforcement business and know just how powerful the government can be. Because of THAT FACT, it didn't take much persuasion when my legal advisors told me to "add a question mark to your title so your book is asking a question rather than making a 'claim' that you can actually 'CURE' anyone of anything." It took me about 2 seconds to say "YES!!!" A question mark by definition is 'a punctuation mark that indicates a question used to express doubt or uncertainty.' And there should <u>ALWAYS</u> be a little bit of 'doubt and uncertainty' about any bold statement such as a "MIRACLE CURE for every disease.

It's always best to question. In fact, I have several small signs around my house that say: "QUESTION EVERYTHING." I placed these small signs to remind myself that having some doubts about everything you read or hear is a VERY GOOD THING. So do question this and all research. **It's good to have some doubts about the things that 'experts' say.** And with that in mind, let me quickly tell you about one of my own personal doubts:

Why I do NOT trust my doctors (and neither should YOU).

I have two doctors that I go to occasionally. Both are nice guys. I like them and always try to make jokes and keep the conversation lively. They have a tough job and I have some a genuine respect for them and what they are <u>trying</u> to do.

But I DO NOT trust them with my health.

It seems to me that all my doctors ever want to do whenever I have gone to see them is a combination of four things: #1: They want to run me through a battery of tests which include sticking cold steel medical devices inside of certain parts of me that nothing should be put into. **#2:** They want to cut me open and do some kind of medical procedure that involves knocking me out. **#3:** Put me in the hospital. (I once spent two weeks in the hospital in a painful procedure called 'traction' for my back. It didn't do any good.) And last, but not least, the favorite thing they want to do — **#4:** DRUG ME!!!

It seems that whenever we go to the doctor, they just want to get us in and out as fast as possible and write us a prescription for some kind of drug. It's the 'chemical solution' for every problem — and I HATE IT!!! I don't know about you, but I do not want to put a bunch of drugs into my body because some doctor didn't know what else to do and wanted to get me out of his office as fast as possible so he or she could get through the roomful of other patients who are waiting. Anyway, one of the things I sometimes joke with my doctors about is the fact that...

In 100 years, they will HAVE A GOOD LAUGH at some of the things that my doctor is doing to me right now!

Yes, it's true. Just like we laugh at some of the CRAZY TREATMENTS that doctors were putting their patients through only a century ago, the people 100 years from now will look at all of the medical treatments that our doctors are SO CONFIDENT about today and have a good laugh! It will be a joke to them... and yet, the joke is on us IF we fully believe in all of the things they are telling us today. In short, just like I think it's a good thing for YOU to 'question' some of everything you hear about your own health (even in this book) — I also sincerely wish that my doctors would 'question' some of their own beliefs... They always seem SO CONFIDENT that all of the drugs and procedures that they prescribe are the only solutions when you and I know that the people in the future will have found solutions that work much better.

Anyway, I believe that because you bought this book, you are OPEN and RECEPTIVE to new ideas and do NOT believe that everything your doctor or all of the other established health professionals tell you is the truth. Even if you like and respect your doctors, I'm sure you recognize the likelihood that in the future, the methods they prescribe to you today will be found obsolete. So if I'm right, and you believe these things, too, then you and I have a lot in common. And I hope that we can meet in person someday to talk about these things.

For now, just keep AN OPEN MIND and read what these experts have to say about the deadly effects of E.B.A. and how to you can combat this terrible problem. In a minute, I'll give you some specific information about the contents in this book and how to get the most out of it.

For now, I want to tell you how the information in this book could potentially make you…

Financially Set For Life!

Would you like to make more money? IF SO, are you searching for a simple and easy way to do it? If you said 'YES!' to both of those questions, then you're in for a real treat! **Because the little-known information in this book is A HIDDEN SECRET in the multi-billion dollar health market that could be worth enormous sums of money to you!**

Yes, it's true. The information in this book is something that millions of people do NOT know anything about. This is the best-kept secret in the multi-billion dollar nutritional supplement industry. And I have discovered and developed a powerful home-based business opportunity that has the power to make you more money than you have ever dreamed possible!

So if you have ever dreamed of being in the right place at the right time and getting involved in an opportunity that has the power to make you huge sums of money, then what I'm about to tell you could be the most exciting information you'll ever receive in your entire life!

Here's what it's all about… As you know, I am NOT a doctor or health practitioner. I'm simply a person who CARES DEEPLY about his health. I spend hundreds of dollars a month on a variety of nutritional supplements and am always searching for the products that will help me LIVE LONGER… have MORE ENERGY… FEEL BETTER… and help me FIGHT all of the deadly diseases such as cancer and heart attacks, etc. **That's how I discovered this powerful information on the deadly situation of EXCESS BODY ACIDITY that many experts call 'The Silent Killer.'** But I wasn't just doing this research for my own personal health… You see, in the back of my mind, I am constantly searching for…

THE PERFECT WAY TO MAKE MONEY!

As I said, I am not an expert in health and nutrition (although by compiling and editing this book, I know SO MUCH MORE about the deadly effects of ACID BUILDUP than most doctors) and yet, what I am is an expert at making huge sums of money! **I am a marketing expert who has spent the last TWO DECADES discovering all of the powerful methods for turning small sums of money into a huge fortune.** The secret to doing this is…

GOOD MARKETING!

If you ask 100 different marketing 'experts' what marketing is, they'll give you 100 different answers. At the end of the day, you'll be even more confused than ever. However, here's my simple to understand definition of what marketing is and ALL of the experts will definitely agree on: **"Marketing is all of the things you do to ATTRACT and RETAIN the highest percentage of the very best prospective buyers for whatever products and/or services you are offering."** It's that simple and yet, attracting and retaining the very best customers in today's world can be very difficult. The market is saturated with too many competitors who are all SHOUTING and SCREAMING at once. The average consumer has MORE

11

CHOICES than ever before and that's a blessing and a curse for those of us in the marketing profession. In short, it's getting harder and harder to attract and retain the very best repeat buyers in any market, but those who are doing the best job at it are making HUGE FORTUNES!

And now YOU can join them!

As I told you earlier, the information you're about to discover in SECTION ONE of this book truly is a 'hidden secret' in the multi-billion dollar health market. And I'm going to show you how it can make you enormous sums of money. Best of all, you'll be helping large numbers of people discover the dangers of EXCESS BODY ACIDITY (E.B.A.) that could actually save their lives! And my company and the powerful marketing system that we have developed can do most or even all of the work for you! Let's talk about BOTH of those amazing benefits. First, **there are tens of millions of people like you and me who CARE DEEPLY about our health, who have never heard of the danger of E.B.A.** This represents a HUGE GAP in the market. And if you've ever wondered if there is a 'secret' to making a lot of money — then you've just found it! In fact, I call 'gaps in the marketplace'...

The #1 SECRET of the world's richest people!

The richest people in the world look for 'gaps in the market' and then fill them with products and services that people go crazy over. They look for unexploited areas: things that people BADLY WANT and are not getting anywhere else. They find these gaps in the market and then fill them with valuable products and services that people go crazy over and they get super rich! Is there more to it than this? YES!!! And yet, the foundation of many fortunes is to find something that people desperately want and are not getting anywhere else — and then give it to them. And this is EXACTLY what we are doing with a new service we have developed called...

'The MIRACLE CURE Advertising and Marketing Service.'

The purpose of this powerful marketing service is to MAKE MONEY by helping millions of people discover the deadly effects of E.B.A. and about our revolutionary products that can COMBAT this 'silent killer.' There are tens of millions of people like you and me who CARE DEEPLY about our health. We want to live longer, be healthier, feel better, and not end up with one of the handful of deadly diseases that are killing millions of people each year. And because we care deeply about all of this, we are constantly on the hunt for NEW INFORMATION that will help us achieve this goal. This is always in the back of our mind all the time. It was in the back of YOUR MIND when you first saw the information about this book. And because tens of millions of people want BETTER HEALTH and a LONGER LIFE that is DISEASE-FREE — and because they're always searching for this, they will be very excited to find out about this information.

You see, even though there is a lot of information on the Internet about E.B.A. (that I used to compile this book), **this is still something that millions of people who care about their health have never heard about.** And because of this, they will be very excited to discover how adding a few revolutionary products to the daily supplements they take now can help them to ELIMINATE the acid build-up in their bodies... restore their pH balance... and experience the optimal health they want more than anything else.

Yes, **millions of people care more about their own health than almost any other thing.** They know that the key to having a happy life is to do all they can to take good care of themselves and they're trying to do this every single day. And the fact that **many of these people have never heard about the deadly effects of E.B.A. spells a HUGE OPPORTUNITY for you and me to make a lot of money.**

Does that sound greedy to you?

Well it's not! **We really are dedicated to helping people get more of the VERY BEST that life has to offer.** And health is the single most important thing. After all, you can have all the money in the world, but if you're sick in a hospital bed or a nursing home, what good will it do you? And you can have the greatest spouse and children and the best friends and family and, yet, if you don't have your health you can't enjoy them in the fullest way and they can't enjoy you. So good health is #1. And when you read SECTION ONE and TWO of this book...

You may be SHOCKED!

Yes, some of the information I have uncovered about the dangers of E.B.A. is absolutely SHOCKING! And although there are some very good books that are already written and lots of great information on the Internet (that you now have in your hands!) — there are millions of people who don't know about the dangers of EXCESS BODY ACIDITY... **Getting involved in our unique business opportunity and marketing service is your chance**

to help these people and help yourself at the same time.

Besides, think about all the billions of dollars being made the big drug companies who develop the latest pills and potions that the medical establishment wants you to take. You can bet they don't think twice about raking in billions of dollars in cash from their latest drugs. They spend millions of dollars on lobbyists and attorneys to defend their ability to sell their little pill and make huge profits. So there's no shame in making money — especially while teaching people about the dangers of Excess Body Acidity and a line of products that really can help people feel better and add life to their years.

Have you ever thought about what it would take to make a lot of money? IF SO, what I'm about to tell you next could make you set for life!

As you know, it's 'GAPS IN THE MARKET' that make people rich. These people simply find profitable areas that are unexploited and fill them with valuable products and services that everyone wants. Again, this is simplistic and there's a lot more to it than that and, yet, this is such a powerful wealth-making principle that I call it "The FOUNDATION of all wealth." You simply must have SOMETHING NEW in an area that many people are already interested in or you'll never be able to hold their attention and interest long enough to tell them how your products or services can help them. **And the information in this book is something new that millions of people are very interested in.** But having a great foundation is just the beginning. It's what you build on that foundation that matters most. And the most powerful and profitable thing you can 'build' on top of that foundation is…

A Proven Marketing System.

As you know, good marketing is the key to wealth. You simply must have something very UNIQUE that people really want. This gives you the power to attract and retain the largest number of the very best prospective buyers. Now all you have to do is have a proven way to attract them. That's what a good marketing system gives you.

This marketing system automatically attracts and retains the very best prospective buyers for whatever you're offering. **A really good marketing system finds the people who are most likely to become your very best**

14

customers, introduces them to your unique products and services (that you know they badly want and need), makes the initial sale to them, and then keeps re-selling them again and again... ALL THIS can be done for you by your powerful marketing system. And if you build the right System for attracting and retaining the largest percentage of repeat buyers...

You can sit back and make money automatically!

A good marketing system will do some or even all of the work for you. It goes out into the marketplace and attracts the people who are most likely to become repeat buyers for your product or service... then it makes the initial sale to them... and then it follows up and makes all of the repeat sales to them. All this can be done for you while you sit back and enjoy the good life.

Does that sound too good to be true?

Maybe.

And yet it is true! I have helped to develop powerful marketing systems that have brought in millions of dollars... and run automatically. It can be VERY DIFFICULT to do all of the initial work to build these marketing systems, but once they are built...

The money can come pouring in
with little or even no work!

As with the other statements in this book — the above headline may sound too good to be true. And it's perfectly okay to have STRONG DOUBTS about all of this! But please keep an open mind. **By my own admission, I am giving you the SHORTCUT VERSION of some of the most powerful marketing discoveries I have made over the last two decades.** There is MUCH MORE to getting rich than the things I have been telling you.

And yet, many average people are now millionaires because they did the two things that I have told you about: **#1:** they found a powerful 'gap' in the market and filled it. And **#2:** They created marketing systems that took care of much or even all of the attraction and retention that are necessary to generate a fortune. Many people have and are doing these things RIGHT NOW as you're reading my words. I know because I am one of them.

I have turned hundreds of dollars into millions of dollars… And my little-known marketing methods have generated tens of millions of dollars in revenue for my little company that's located in the tiny town of Goessel, Kansas… And my all new 'MIRACLE CURE Advertising and Marketing Service' is a powerful method that has the powerful potential to generate a HUGE FORTUNE for you!

My wife, Eileen, and I started with only $300.00 in 1988 and we quickly turned it into $500.00 a day… Then we met marketing expert Russ von Hoelscher and thanks to his help, support, and guidance, we went from $16,000.00 a month to almost $100,000.00 a week! And we did this in just 9 months!

It's true. We went from $16,000.00 a month to almost $100,000.00 a week — thanks to the little-known marketing and advertising methods that Russ taught us. And since then, we have been fine-tuning and testing and tweaking all of our methods and have used them to generate tens of millions of dollars. Within our first 5 years, we had brought in a grand total of $10,000,000.00!

Yes, millions and millions of dollars have came pouring in thanks to the amazing little known secrets that we have discovered since 1988. **And now we have taken the best-of-the-best of all of these rare and unusual marketing methods and put them all into our new 'MIRACLE CURE Advertising and Marketing Service.'** As you'll see, this is designed to let you make huge sums of money with the very best of all the methods we have ever discovered and we do it all for you! Yes, you simply sit back… relax… and let us take care of everything for you. We do it all for you — including the powerful, but TRUE FACT that…

We spend ALL of our own money on ALL of the complicated and expensive marketing that must be done to make YOU the largest sum of money!

It's true! As you'll discover, our entire marketing process is somewhat complex. In other words, it has taken us MANY YEARS TO MASTER and there are a lot of steps to it. But you don't have to worry about any of that because we take care of everything for you! And because you will be our Joint Venture Business Partner and because we make money for helping you make money — then we will do all we can to see to it that you get paid the largest sum of money in the fastest time and for the longest period of time!

Yes, our success is directly tied to yours! So the more we do to make sure that you get paid the largest sum of money, the more money we are also making for ourselves...

 So please go over SECTION FOUR of this book very carefully. This section gives you some of the MAIN ADVANTAGES of our powerful and proven 'MIRACLE CURE Advertising and Marketing Service.' **We have identified some of the major problems that you'll face with most businesses and then we show you how our 'MIRACLE CURE Advertising and Marketing Service' solves these problems.** This is very important because you can never understand how valuable something is until, and unless, you have SOMETHING ELSE to compare it to. I can tell you all day long that our advertising and management service is one of the greatest business opportunities in the world — BUT YOU'D EXPECT ME TO SAY THAT!

 You know I am biased. So I decided to let YOU prove this to yourself, by telling you about the VERY SPECIFIC PROBLEMS that you will face in most businesses and then show you how our unique business opportunity ELIMINATES these problems. This will help to OPEN YOUR EYES to the potential problems you'll face if you choose to get involved in another business. Plus, it will give you A DEEPER UNDERSTANDING of just how valuable our 'MIRACLE CURE Advertising and Marketing Service' really is.

 As with all of the information in this book, your goal is to question everything for yourself. So please make the time to carefully go through this book. As you'll see, this is unlike any book you have probably ever seen. For example, the first two sections are simply a combination of SMALL ARTICLES. They are in no particular order and many of them contain some of the same basic information. Because of this...

You do not have to read this book from cover to cover!

 Instead, you can SKIM THROUGH IT again and again and gain important new information every time you do!

 The information in this book really can save your life! It can lead to better health that will add years to your life and life to your years. I hope you enjoy reading it half as much as my staff and I enjoyed compiling and editing it. This information has been SHOCKING to us. **We are now deeply committed to restoring our pH balance and living a disease-free life. I'm hoping that you will be, too.**

So please spend some time skimming through Sections One, Two, and Three of this book to familiarize yourself with the deadly dangers of EXCESS BODY ACIDITY and then go on to Section Four and discover how our unique business opportunity solves many of the MAIN PROBLEMS that you'll have in other businesses. Then take the NEXT STEP and get started with us at once! Just follow the simple and easy instructions in the back of this book. As you will (hopefully) see, **this has the power to make you huge sums of money** while helping the millions of people who do not know about this 'miracle cure' for every disease. **I'll look forward to meeting you in person and hearing you tell me how this information has helped to save your life and is making you set for life!**

SECTION ONE:

The Cure for All Disease?

Only One Disease and One Cure.

Excess acidity is a condition that weakens all body systems.

Excess acidity forces the body to borrow minerals — including sodium, calcium, potassium, and magnesium from vital organs and bones to buffer (neutralize) the acid and to safely remove it from the body. As a result, the body can suffer severe and prolonged 'corrosion' due to high acidity — a condition that may go undetected for years.

It affects virtually every person in our society because of the way we live, the way we eat, the way we think, and the environment believe in. The result is an internal environment where disease can easily manifest, as opposed to a pH-balanced environment which allows for normal body functions necessary for the body to resist disease. It is true that if we have a healthy body, we will maintain sufficient alkaline reserves to meet emergency demands.

However when excess acids must be continually neutralized, our alkaline reserves are depleted, leaving the body in a weakened, disease prone condition.

Unfortunately, there are still many practitioners who believe that the body can some how miraculously and 'naturally' balance its pH — as if we were living in nature and eating raw foods and herbs. The truth is so far beyond this ideal.

The truth, according to Dr Lynda Frassetto, acid/alkaline researcher from the University of California, is that we have turned an evolutionary corner.

We simply do not handle acid waste the way we used to.

Her research showed the sheer volume of acid waste our body has to handle has forced it to take drastic 'war' style action to preserve its strategic reserves: the kidney and liver our major essential detoxifying organs.

In her study of almost 1,000 aging subjects, she found that we are now 'stock piling' acid in fatty deposits rather than eliminating it via the kidneys and liver.

When excess acids must be continually neutralized, our alkaline reserves are depleted, leaving the body in a weakened, disease prone condition.

21

In its infinite wisdom, the body has chosen to save the kidney and liver from degradation by excess acid.

Of course, there is a cost. It's called obesity, lowered immunity, lack of energy and the whole host of acid related diseases we are subject to including cancer, diabetes, osteoarthritis and more — much, much more.

Acid Alkaline HISTORY

The concept of acid/alkaline imbalance as the cause of disease isn't a new one.

One of the first persons who talked about the need to alkalize the body was the great "Sleeping Prophet" Edgar Cayce.

He always referred to body detoxification with herbs, colonics, fasting, massage, steam baths, and diet modification with the aim of alkalizing the body.

Way back in 1933 Dr. William Howard Hay published a ground-breaking book, *A New Health Era*, in which he maintained that all disease is caused by 'autotoxication' (or "self- poisoning") due to acid accumulation in the body: "Now we depart from health in just the proportion to which we have allowed our alkalis to be dissipated by introduction of acid-forming food in too great amount...

It may seem strange to say that all disease is the same thing, no matter what its myriad modes of expression, but it is verily so.

More recently, in his remarkable book, *'Alkalize or Die'*, Dr. Theodore A. Baroody said essentially the same thing:

"The countless names of illnesses do not really matter. What does matter is that they all come from the same root cause... too much tissue acid waste in the body!"

Dr. Robert O. Young, Ph.D. in his book, *'The pH Miracle'* says it this way: "Those willing to look again, and with clear eyes, will be rewarded with the secrets to permanent health. We can heal ourselves by changing the environment inside our bodies. Potentially harmful invaders, then, will have nowhere to grow and will become harmless."

Unfortunately, according to Sang Whang, author of *Reverse Aging* even

It may seem strange to say that all disease is the same thing, no matter what its myriad modes of expression, but it is verily so.

The countless names of illnesses do not really matter. What does matter is that they all come from the same root cause... too much tissue acid waste in the body!

if we eat the best of organic fruit and vegetables, 97% of our food still consists of carbon, nitrogen, hydrogen, and oxygen, which will still be reduced to acid waste.

He says that it is not what we put into our bodies, it is what stays in our bodies as waste that creates our over-acidic condition and what causes us to age prematurely.

Sang Whang says that in terms of acid/alkaline balance, the only difference between 'good' food and 'bad food' is that 'good' food will have less acid waste and more acid neutralizing result.

Your pH balance depends on what is left after metabolism. So we'll take a look in this article at what foods, lifestyles, and supplements contribute to a 'clean' house within.

Here our metabolism can operate as it is supposed to instead of acting as a continual janitor in an increasingly overloaded toxic warehouse.

Leftover Acid Waste

Very few, if any, of us are physically capable of ridding our bodies of all the acids we create from food, stress, and our own metabolism. These acid wastes move around the body via the blood and lymphatic system until our overloaded kidneys decide to dump them or us within, as the body struggles to counteract acid-producing foods, acid producing pollution and acid-producing stress. In fact of all acidifying factors, stress is the greatest. It can neutralize and acidify an alkaline diet with one surge of the acidic hormone adrenalin.

Long Term Acidity Is Like Rust

It corrodes our tissue, eating into our 96,000 kilometers of veins and arteries. Left unchecked, it eventually interrupts all cellular activities and functions, from the beating of the heart to the way we think.

As we have mentioned, acids can be stored in fat. Cholesterol and crystallized uric acid are solidified acids that have been dumped within the body for 'later' removal — the 'later' that never comes.

It is not what we put into our bodies, it is what stays in our bodies as waste that creates our over-acidic condition.

Acid Effects

Acid coagulates blood. Blood has major problems flowing around fatty acids.

32 glasses of neutral pH water are needed to balance one glass of Cola.

Capillaries clog up and die. The skin, deprived of life-giving healthy blood, loses elasticity and begins to wrinkle.

Even with a face lift or liposuction, the acid remains and continues its relentless advance. Without a basic acid/alkaline balancing plan, every part of your body works ever harder to maintain health because every system; all the organs, the lungs, even the skin are involved in the maintenance of correct blood pH.

The War Within

Within your body, your organs and cells are totally subservient to your blood. All organs work to keep your blood at a balanced pH, to the point where your body is willing to inflict major damage on organs if they appear to stand in the way of correct blood pH. If its pH drops from its optimum pH 7.365 down to pH 6.95, you will lapse into a coma and die.

"...we have turned an evolutionary corner "

That's why you get such a charge from a can of Cola. Its pH of 2.5 acidity sets alarm bells ringing all over your body.

Over-acidification interferes with life itself leading to virtually all sickness and disease!

Alkaline chemical stores that should be used elsewhere are sacrificed to the call of the adrenalin that floods your system.

The 'high' you have learned to expect is no different from the high a drug user experiences as his artificial sensory elevates. It is your body screaming "Help" and you enjoying the thrill of the fear. It's "The Real thing."

It's not just a glass of Cola that causes such effect. (32 glasses of neutral pH water are needed to balance one glass of Cola). Most of us already have a running battle.

In summary, over-acidification interferes with life itself leading to virtually all sickness and disease! Finally, it ages then kills us.

When we die, it celebrates by turning the whole body acid giving birth to antagonistic micro-organisms to the party!

Dr. Baroody expresses it very well: "Too much acidity in the body is like having too little oil in the car."

It just grinds to a halt one lazy Sunday afternoon. There you are — stuck.

The body does the same thing. It starts creaking to a stop along the byways of life and you find yourself in some kind of discomfort. "I watch with great concern as people of all classes and lifestyles suffer from this excess."

He attributes no less than 68 major health conditions to a prior existent acidic inner terrain.

Why Are Westerners So Prone To Obesity?

Is it just food? Of course, the food we eat, its quantity and quality has a large effect on our waist measurement.

But because the body has made a habit of its 'last chance' solution (pirating calcium from the bones and teeth) of what to do with excess toxic acid waste, there is another reason we deposit fat.

As Dr. Frassetto discovered, when we are faced with shortage of options due to an acid besieged inner terrain, we dump toxic wastes in fatty deposits as far away from the organs and heart as possible: on the buttocks, the chest, the thighs and the belly.

When we are faced with shortage of options due to an acid besieged inner terrain, we dump toxic wastes in fatty deposits as far away from the organs and heart as possible.

Dr Robert O. Young writes convincingly on the same subject. He sees sugar as anacid and as the reason we are so fat, but not as we have been taught. He says that the body has to protect itself from the excess sugar we consume, and so it co-ops fat to encase it and protect us from it.

"Fat is saving our lives." — Dr Robert O. Young

Alkalinity and Energy levels

Acidity or alkalinity of our internal fluids has a profound effect even at the individual cellular level.

MITOCHONDRIA: THE BODY'S CELLULAR POWER PLANT

In our bodies our entire metabolic process is dependent upon balance, right down to the cellular level. Our 75 trillion cells are mildly alkaline within, dependent on our inner sea — the surrounding alkaline interstitial fluid to surround them.

Without this relationship, no useful chemical or energy interchange will occur because no pH balance exists. pH opposites — acid and alkaline — in the body are the chemical method for electricity to flow. Without sufficient 'polarity' between the interior of the cell and the fluid surrounding it, the energy of the cell has difficulty flowing into the surrounding tissues.

Weight loss and the regaining of energy occurs more easily when we take the first steps towards an alkaline 'rebalance'.

Alkalinity and Your Blood

Blood is always slightly alkaline (or at least it should be!). As the only transport system for nutrients to every part of your body, blood cannot afford to be acidic. It needs to stay within a pH range that will maintain resistance to decay or putrefaction, and the birth of malevolent micro-organisms. Hence pH 7.365 is the ideal environment in which micro-organisms remain in co-existent or symbiotic harmony with the body.

Allow the blood to shift slightly either way and results will be felt in every part of the body. Microforms sustained by an acidic environment begin to multiply and mutate taking the form of aggressive, parasitic, and pathogenic agents.

Scientists studying live blood using phase constast microscopy can see the changes in the blood taking place and correlate it with the progression of the disease process.

They witness a repetitive pattern unfolding that has prompted them to state that the over-acidification of the body, caused by improper eating, thinking and living, causes a biological transformation of matter into microforms which debilitates or recycles the body and, if no corrected, may ultimately cause our demise.

The Real Power of pH

If any substance changes from pH 7 to pH 8, it has become ten times more alkaline.

Conversely, if it has changes from neutral pH 7 to pH 6, it is 10 times

---

Blood needs to stay within a pH range that will maintain resistance to decay or putrefaction, and the birth of malevolent micro-organisms.

Microforms sustained by an acidic environment begin to multiply and mutate, taking the form of aggressive, parasitic, and pathogenic agents.

more acidic. As an example, a popular Cola, at pH 2.5 is almost 50,000 times more acidic than neutral water, and needs 32 glasses of neutral (pH 7) water to counteract the consumption of one glass of Cola. (Active ingredient: Phosphoric Acid)

You can now see that a change from the normal level 7.365 to pH 7 would mean that your blood would suddenly be around 4 times as acid as it should be. You would die from poisoning by your own blood.

This is why every body system is used to support the correct blood pH.

You can also understand from this that our blood pH can be affected at any time of the day by a myriad of events: food, drink, stress, pollution, exercise, or beneficially by meditation, by drinking alkaline water, by deep breathing, even by being happy.

A change from the normal level 7.365 to pH 7 would mean that your blood would suddenly be around 4 times as acid as it should be. You would die from poisoning by your own blood.

You Never Have to Get Sick!

Maintaining the alkaline pH of the saliva, urine, tears, sweat, and blood is critical. Testing the body fluid pH is the most important daily measurement anyone can do to maintain health and fitness and to PREVENT ALL sickness and disease. The beauty of the pH test is that you don't need to go to a doctor to do it. You can do it yourself. You can actually become your own doctor and manage your own health with this simple test. And if you'll remember this rule: if you maintain the saliva and the urine pH, ideally at 7.2 or above, you will never get sick.

That's right you will NEVER get sick!

The key is to manage the alkaline design of the body fluids. But most people on the planet have a urine or saliva pH in the six or fives. They don't manage their pH. People take better care of their aquariums, swimming pools, or spas, than their own internal body fluids.

Managing the pH of your body fluids is simple. All you do is take some pHydrion paper or litmus paper, moisten it with saliva and urine and then check the color on the color-coded chart. The chart measures the pH of saliva, urine, sweat, and tears in 5.0 to 8.5 increments.

Ideally, you want your saliva, urine, sweat and tears to measure at least 7.2 or better. Managing you body fluid pH with an alkaline lifestyle and diet is the healthiest advice I could give anyone on this planet. It is inexpensive. It is simple, and it works.

QUESTION: When these body fluids stay acidic for days, weeks, months, or years, what happens to human health?

ANSWER: What happens to human health when you stay in the acidic zone? You get sick, tired, and fat. And, if you don't get fat, you die. When you are underweight you are living on your own body tissue. Your body is making red blood cells out of body cells. Why? Because you have damaged the root system of your small intestine with acidic food, drink, enzymes, probiotics, antibiotics, and other acidic drugs. You are constantly breaking down your own body cells in order to maintain the level of red blood cells at 5 million red blood cells per cubic millimeter.

In order to build muscle and bones you have to have healthy strong red blood cells. In order to have healthy strong red blood cells you have to have a healthy alkaline

If you maintain the saliva and the urine pH, ideally at 7.2 or above, you will never get sick.

29

root system or intestinal villi with an alkaline lifestyle and diet. You build healthy blood with electron-rich green alkaline foods and drinks. When you are constantly bombarding your internal environment with acidic foods and drinks and damaging your intestinal villi, you set the stage for all sickness and dis-ease.

When we ingest any acidic food or drink, our body immediately reacts to neutralize or buffer the acid. For example, let's say you drink a glass of orange juice. But before drinking the orange juice you test the pH of your saliva. After drinking the orange juice you test your saliva pH again. You would think that drinking orange juice, which has a pH between 2.5 to 3 and is highly acidic, would actually cause the pH of your saliva to go down. But it does not.

The saliva pH goes up higher then when you first tested the pH. The pH of the saliva should test out over 8. What is happening is the salivary glands are releasing sodium bicarbonate to buffer the acids of the orange juice. This is why the saliva pH goes up. If the saliva pH does not go up this indicates that your alkaline reserves are deficient. All forms of sugar are acidic to the body. Even fruit sugars are acidic. When the body is trying to neutralize an acid, it has to secrete an alkaline buffer to do so.

When you ingest sugar or you drink a glass of fresh orange juice, or you take any acidic food in the mouth, the pH will sharply go up to neutralize the acid from that food. This is done to protect the alkaline design of the body. When you start using up your alkaline reserves and you do not replace those reserves with alkaline foods and drinks, you begin to compromise other parts of the body. Especially if, the daily diet is loaded with acidic foods and drinks. When the alkaline reserves are deficient and the diet is also deficient in foods or drinks that will build up those alkaline reserves the body starts pulling alkaline minerals from the bones and muscles. This causes deficiencies of the bones and muscles.

When your blood is compromised from a deficiency of alkaline reserves, such as sodium bicarbonate or the elements to make sodium bicarbonate, the body will begin pulling calcium from the bones and/or magnesium from the muscles to maintain the alkalinity of the blood plasma. This is when you will start experiencing the deficiencies of alkalinity that are expressed in the seven stages of acidosis, going from sensitivities all the way up to degeneration.

When you are alkalized you are energized. And when you are energized you feel better and think better. You have sustainable energy when you are alkalized. When you eat and drink alkaline you are making energy deposits to your body, like a bank account. You are making alkaline deposits to your energy bank account and to your alkaline reserves or energy savings account. The positive benefits of being alkaline are incredible health, energy, fitness, mental clarity, and vitality.

Why is balancing your pH so important?

Balancing your pH is important because it is based on a foundational health principal that the human body is alkaline by design, but every function of the body is acidic. So every disease is nothing more than the body trying to maintain its alkaline design. So when we're talking about bone disease, the body is taking alkalinity from the bones to maintain the alkalinity of the blood, which is the most important part of the body. Once the blood becomes acidic, you will die.

A drop from the normal blood pH of 7.365 to 6.9 will cause one to go into a coma and then die. The blood pH has a very narrow range for health and vitality. The normal healthy blood pH is at 7.365. If the blood pH drops down to 7.2, you start feeling very sick and at 6.9 you are dead. So the body will do everything it can to maintain the alkaline integrity of the blood at the expense of all other organs and organ systems.

Once we understand this foundational theory, and I'll repeat it again: the human organism is alkaline by design, although acidic by function. So breathing is acidic. Thinking is acidic. Eating is acidic. Metabolism is acidic. The breakdown of the food you eat is acidic. Everything you eat is acidic to a lesser or greater degree. The body has to protect itself. The body protects itself with the alkaline buffering system which is currently NOT understood by medical savants.

Your body is looking for energy in the form of electrons or electron-rich foods and drinks. Health is all about energy. We need to realize the foundational principles of health, fitness, and energy and how to maintain that health, fitness, and energy, for a lifetime, free from ALL sickness and disease.

True immunity from ALL sickness and disease comes from alkalinity not from white blood cells. We were all taught in human biology that immunity comes from white blood cells protecting us from some invading germ or virus. White blood cells provide NO immunity. White blood cells do not destroy germs. White blood cells are glorified janitors that swim around in our blood and lymphatic plasma picking up the garbage we create from an acidic lifestyle and diet. White

A drop from the normal blood pH of 7.365 to 6.9 will cause one to go into a coma and then die.

True immunity from ALL sickness and disease comes from alkalinity not from white blood cells.

31

blood cells are NOT soldiers, destroying some invading germ coming in from the outside world that would make us sick.

The first line of defense against sickness and disease is an alkaline internal environment.

Germs DO NOT cause disease. Acids cause pain, sickness and disease.

True immunity comes to each of us by maintaining the alkaline fluids of the body. That is where true immunity is found. The first line of defense against sickness and disease is an alkaline internal environment. As soon as you put something acidic into your mind, into your mouth, into your lungs, your alkaline buffering system is engaged to neutralizing or buffer any acidic food, drink, or thought that might be present. That's true immunity. It is found in the alkaline reserves for your body. When you have an alkaline lifestyle and diet you are able to defend off environmental, dietary, or metabolic acids that would make you sick, tired, and/or fat.

Germs DO NOT cause disease. Acids cause pain, sickness and disease. There is a simple way to understand this principal. Let's compare our bodies to an automobile. When you start your car, the car begins using energy. As the car uses energy is creates an acidic waste product called carbon monoxide. When you turn the car off you stop producing this acid. If you start the car again and stuff a few socks or a potato in the tailpipe the car will die from carbon monoxide acidosis. If you were to stop eliminating your own acidic

waste products through urination, perspiration, defecation, or respiration, like the car, you would die too.

The body has a way of protecting itself from excess acidity. When dietary and/or metabolic acids are not properly eliminated they get parked on your hips, thighs, buttocks, waistline, breasts, and brain. The body does this to protect and preserve the organs and organ systems that sustain life. Your best immunity to protect your body from ALL sickness and disease DOES NOT come from vaccination or medication. True immunity comes from protecting the alkaline design of the body with an alkaline lifestyle and diet. Once again, white blood cells, including neutrophils, eosinophils, basophils, T and B-cells help to maintain cleanliness, and in reality are just the janitors of your body fluids like an automatic pool sweep. You can support your white blood cells with an electron-rich alkaline lifestyle and diet.

Bacteria and yeast are biological transformations of what used to be organized matter from healthy body cells. You know if you leave food in the back of the refrigerator that it will spoil. And, if you leave it long enough it will give birth to first bacteria, then yeast and finally mold. You know that food is not infected from the outside world, but is spoiling from the inside out.

Bacteria, yeast, and mold are nothing more than a biological transformation of matter. You can accept this. But for some reason, science has adopted a medical philosophy or theory that somehow germs are species-specific, as if they're individual like a cat or a dog. There is nothing special about a virus or bacteria. A virus is nothing more than a smaller bacterial form, from disorganizing or transforming matter. A virus, is many times just crystallized acids. When you look at bacteria under the microscope, what you are looking at are fragments of what used to be a brain cell or a bone cell or blood cell.

And, yeast is just another transformation or evolution, very similar to looking at a caterpillar transforming later into a beautiful butterfly. You accept the reality that the butterfly, use to be a different form—it use to be a caterpillar and now is a beautiful butterfly. And yet this idea of attaching some sort of identity to germs has become very popular over the last 150 years. And the whole focus of medical science has been trying to figure out how to kill the virus, bacteria, yeast, or mold. And yet, in reality, the germ is nothing more than a transformation of matter. You cannot kill matter you can only change matter. Because matter cannot be created nor can it be destroyed, it can only change its former function.

So therefore, bacteria, yeast, and mold is nothing more than a biological transformation of matter that has taken place because of an environment that has become acidic. When the internal environment becomes acidic, the body or blood cell will change. When you take water and put it in the freezer, it turns to ice. When you take water and put it on the stove, it turns to steam. Nothing is ever lost, and nothing is ever gained. The matter is still there, it just takes on a different form. This is a law of physics.

When you see bacteria and yeast in the body, all you are looking at is the transformation of what use to be a body cell, a red blood cell, a white blood cell, or a heart cell, and that bacteria or yeast is the evidence of a compromised internal acidic environment. Germs DO NOT cause disease; they are the expression that the internal environment is acidic. You see, the great germ theory of medical science is a scientific illusion.

The Germ is Nothing! The Alkaline Internal Environment is Everything!

The easiest way for someone to check and maintain the body fluid pH is to test the urine and saliva.

The best time to test the urine is in the morning because the morning urine is an expression of what you

Bacteria and yeast are biological transformations of what used to be organized matter from healthy body cells.

There is nothing special about a virus or bacteria. A virus is nothing more than a smaller bacterial form, from disorganizing or transforming matter. A virus, is many times just crystallized acids.

ate and what you drank and how you lived your life the previous 24 hours. The morning urine is not a product of the blood; it is a product of the tissues. When you measure your urine, you are measuring the pH of your tissues. If your pH is below the ideal of 7.2, and it measures in the 5's or 6's, you are in tissue acidosis.

When someone over-exercises they can go into lactic tissue acidosis. Lactic acid from over-exercise is felt in the connective tissues and muscles. When the muscles are sore, that's the tissues picking up the acid to maintain the alkaline blood pH. The blood has to rid itself of metabolic acids or you would die. So it throws the acid out into the muscle tissues and you feel it as irritation or inflammation. If the lactic acid stays in the tissues, it will spoil the tissue cells, and the body will go into preservation mode.

In preservation mode, the body will encapsulate the cells spoiled by lactic acid, and now you have a tumor. The tumor is the solution to stop systemic spoiling or metastasis. When the lymphatic system is healthy it will pull the lactic acid out of the tissues, and eventually you will sweat it out or it will be recycled back into the blood and you will urinate it out. So this is very, very important. So remember, when you are testing the pH of your urine, you are testing the pH of your tissues.

And when you are testing your saliva, you are testing your ability or potential to alkalize your food and drink. So when you're saliva pH is below 7.2, your potential for alkalizing your food, drink, and emotions is less. Your reserves are low. You need to make a deposit to your alkaline bank account. And that would be the same with your urine. When your urine is acidic, you need to start alkalizing. You run the risk of staying within an acidic zone; you run the risk of going through the seven stages of acidosis. Starting with lack of energy to sensitivities to inflammation, and working up to ulceration and degeneration.

Every doctor, hospital, nutritionist, health care professional should be using pHydrion paper to monitor their patients' body fluids. They should be giving pHydrion paper to their patients so they can monitor their tissue pH. *Doctors need to educate NOT medicate*. My goal is to empower every individual person on the planet to be able to take responsibility for their own health and fitness.

The fishbowl metaphor.

The fishbowl metaphor is very simple to understand and it starts out with a question. Here is the question. "If the fish is sick, what would you do? Would you treat the fish or change the water?" If you said change the water you are correct. When you put on your common-sense hat and you ask this question, "If the fish is sick, what would you do? Treat the fish or change that water?" Right off the top of your head, you would say, "I would change the water."

If you ask the same question to your doctor, what would you expect? "Well, I'd treat the fish." Because that's what doctors do. That's their mindset. But when you realize that every cell in the body is eternal in nature, and would live forever if you would only maintain the correct alkaline pH, you see, there would be no aging of the body. I mean, in a perfect scenario. But, we don't live in a perfect scenario. Ideally, in the perfect scenario, the life expectancy of the human cell, that makes up all of your organs and tissues are infinite.

Every day you either choose to live or you choose to die — either by omission or commission. Either you do it with knowledge or you do it with a lack of knowledge. When you have a lack of knowledge, you live in acidic state and you can end up sick, tired, and/or fat. It is critical for me to tell you that "YES, testing your urine and saliva is the most important thing one can do to maintain the body in an alkaline state full of health, fitness, vitality, hope, love, and peace." You'll be surprised at how healthy, energetic, and strong you will get, even when everyone around you is getting sick. That just won't happen to you anymore!

Alkaline foods add electrons to the body.

Alkaline foods are full of electrons or electrical energy. This is the energy the body runs on. Electrons NOT calories. Alkaline foods and drinks wouldn't be alkaline if they didn't have electrons. That's what makes them alkaline. In the duality of life there needs to be opposition in all things that we might learn by our experience. It is through free agency, our life choices that we learn and grow and experience the unique differences between sickness and disease and health and vitality.

The pH scale is a scientific measurement of the energy of the food or drink. The pH stands for the potential of hydrogen (H+) or proton concentration in a aqueous solution. The pH scale also measures the potential of hydroxyl ions (OH-) or electron concentration any food or drink that is alkaline is going to be saturated with hydroxyl ion or electrons.

Let me give you an example for illustration purposes. When you go to the store to purchase batteries, do you purchase alkaline/electron rich batteries or do you purchase acidic/proton rich batteries? I know you know the answer. Remember the Ever Ready Battery Bunny who keeps on running and running and running? The reason the Bunny keeps on running is because he is an alkaline bunny saturated with electrons. When you purchase batteries for a flashlight you purchase the alkaline/electron rich batteries because they are full of energy. When batteries die or have no life, they're acidic and saturated with protons. The same is true with the human body.

When the body is full of alkalinity or electrons we are full of energy and life. When the body becomes acidic and saturated with protons we have little or no energy. I measure the food or drink with an alkaline electron meter to determine which foods and drinks have energy and which foods and drinks do not. Many foods will pull energy from the body and these are the foods which are highly acidic. Such as coffee, tea, alcohol, dairy, and animal protein.

If you want energy, then you need to saturate your body with electron-rich alkaline foods and drinks. It is that simple. The body runs on electrons not protons. The body is electrical and it doesn't run on calories. When you are looking to power up your body, like you would power up a car, I hope you use the best fuel. And, the best kind of fuel to power up the body is electron-rich alkaline foods, such as

broccoli, spinach, cucumber, avocado, celery, parsley, kale, okra, just to name a few.

Alkaline foods become an antioxidant.

All alkaline foods and drinks are saturated with antioxidants that buffer the acids of digestion, metabolism, and the external environment. The word "antioxidant" was coined several years ago by a pharmaceutical company to market their drugs. It is a word to describe some of the phytochemicals or nutrients they had isolated for buffering free radicals.

Several scientists have suggested that free radicals or reactive oxygen species were damaging body cells and causing cancer. In truth, the antioxidant is nothing more than an agent of energy or electron that buffers dietary and metabolic acidity. And, any agent that buffers acidity is going to be an antioxidant which allows for an internal environment to be more oxygenated or alkaline. Dietary and metabolic acids create more of an environment that's oxygen-deprived, so this word antioxidant has become very, very popular. But, I do not believe that people really understand what antioxidant means. It's not that it's against oxygenation, it's against oxidants, and oxidants are things that rust or break down the body. Oxidants are acids!

Anything that rusts, ferments, or breaks down the body is an acid. So anything we can do to neutralize ferments or acids is good and healthful to the body. Using antioxidants, such as glutathione, N-acetyl-Cysteine, luctein, pycnogenol, Vitamin D, E, and F, will buffer or neutralize the toxic ferment or acid and this would be a positive thing for keeping the body young, healthy, and energized.

Acidic foods take electrons away from our body.

Acidic foods steals electrons and energy from your body. This is what happens when we eat proton-rich acidic foods. Whether it is chicken, eggs, dairy, bread, or any form of sugar they will pull energy from your body rather than contribute energy to our body. A continued use of proton-rich acidic foods or drinks will eventually make you tired, sick, and then dead!

Do not be fooled by the drug and food companies. Most drug and food companies are marketing drugs, foods, and liquids that will eventually shorten your life, increase your addiction, and bring you pain, sorrow, and a miserable death.

Disease is the state of imbalance in the body that is brought on by an inverted way of living, eating, and thinking. All disease is caused by individual choice. You do not get sick without making acidic lifestyle and dietary choices. When you choose to eat acidic foods or drink, such as animal flesh or dairy products like cheese, you set yourself up for a serious health challenge, such as breast cancer for a woman or prostate cancer for a man.

This statement was made over 25 years ago that all sickness and disease is a result of an inverted way of living, eating, and thinking. It is critical to understand the foundational principle of good health. The foundational principal of understanding is knowing that the human body is alkaline by design and acidic by function. When you understand that the body needs to be maintained in an alkaline state in order to have sustainable energy, health, and vitality, then everything you drink, everything you eat, every activity you engage in, even your thoughts, must be alkaline. Your health, energy, and vitality, is an expression of what we're eating, what you're drinking and what you are thinking.

If you are eating an acidic diet, that's creating internal acidic pollution, and a breakdown or fermentation of body cells, this of course, will lead to a host of all types of disease conditions. There are seven stages of disease or acidity. I have said there is only one sickness and one disease? The one sickness and one disease is the over-

Anything that rusts, ferments, or breaks down the body is an acid. So anything we can do to neutralize ferments or acids is good and healthful to the body.

The foundational principal of understanding is knowing that the human body is alkaline by design and acidic by function.

Disease is the state of imbalance in the body that is brought on by an inverted way of living, eating, and thinking.

The one sickness and one disease is the over-acidification of the blood and then tissues due to an inverted way of living, thinking, and eating.

All degenerative conditions are caused by environmental, dietary and/or metabolic acids, such as osteoporosis, MS and ALL cancers.

The standard American diet is 100% acid. It is the major cause of ALL disease.

acidification of the blood and then tissues due to an inverted way of living, thinking and eating. This one disease and one sickness has seven stages or seven expressions, which have been categorized by medical science as in different types of diseases. But there are NOT many diseases only one disease and one health!

For example, cancer is part of that one disease. MS is part of that one disease. Heart disease and diabetes are also part of the one disease. Allergies, arthritis, osteoporosis, bowel restrictions-congestions, from diverticulitis to diverticulosis, Crohn's, all of these diseases are the result of a compromised alkaline design through individual acidic lifestyle and dietary choice.

The seven stages of disease or acidity are as follows:

1. The first stage of acidosis is enervation.

2. The second stage of acidosis is sensitivities and irritation.

3. The third stage of acidosis the third is catarrh or mucus buildup.

4. The fourth stage is inflammation.

5. The fifth stage in indurations or fibrotic tissue or

hardening of the arteries.

6. The sixth stage is ulceration such as in an ulcerated liver, stomach, or bowels.

7. And the seventh stage of acidosis is degeneration.

All degenerative conditions are caused by environmental, dietary, and/or metabolic acids, such as osteoporosis, MS, and ALL cancers.

But whatever the disease condition, there's only one cause. And, that one cause is excess-acidity from lifestyle and dietary choice that compromises your internal environment, that then leads to a breakdown of your body cells and tissues. You will feel your stage of acidity. You will eventually sit down to the banquet of your lifestyle and dietary choices. There is NO escape!

The standard American diet is 100% acid. It is the major cause of ALL disease. It is at the foundation of the American health crisis. It is the reason so many are sick, tired, and dying. It is the reason diabetes, cancer, and heart disease is on the rise. It is the major cause of family and national economic bankruptcy. The nation is looking for change. The change we need must include education NOT medication. Prevention is the cure for disease NOT treatment. True prevention comes with an electron-rich alkaline lifestyle and diet. There is NO other way. The diet in America and around the world must change from an acidic lifestyle and diet to an alkaline diet. I would suggest at least 80% alkaline and 20% acidic.

What is Alkalinity?

Alkalinity is the buffering capacity of a water body. It measures the ability of water bodies to neutralize acids and bases thereby maintaining a fairly stable pH. Water that is a good buffer contains compounds such as bicarbonates, carbonates, and hydroxides, which combine with H+ ions from the water thereby raising the pH (more basic) of the water. Without this buffering capacity, any acid added to a lake would immediately change its pH.

Why is alkalinity important?

Aquatic organisms benefit from a stable pH value in their optimal range. To maintain a fairly constant pH in a water body, a higher alkalinity is preferable. High alkalinity means that the water body has the ability to neutralize acidic pollution from rainfall or basic inputs from wastewater. A well buffered lake also means that daily fluctuations of CO_2 concentrations (discussed above) result in only minor changes in pH throughout the course of a day.

What affects alkalinity?

Alkalinity comes from rocks and soils, salts, certain plant activities, and certain industrial wastewater discharges (detergents and soap-based products are alkaline). If an area's geology contains large quantities of calcium carbonate ($CaCO_3$, limestone), water bodies tend to be more alkaline. Granite bedrock (much of RI) is deficient in alkaline materials to buffer acidic inputs.

Addition of lime as a soil amendment to decrease acidity in home lawns can runoff into surface waters and increase alkalinity.

Alkalinity and Your Body

Alkalinity, referred to as the pH, is determined by the concentration of Hydrogen ions in a substance such as water, blood, or food. On a scale from 1 — 14, a pH level of 7.0 is considered neutral, 7.0 downwards is increasingly acidic and upwards of 7.0 is increasingly alkaline. Our bodies are alkaline by design and acidic by function. God made the body so that both components are needed. The human body has adapted to two types of digestion, alkaline for starches and acid for proteins, but true health lives in an alkaline state.

How do we get alkaline and why should we care? We can get

Prevention is the cure for disease NOT treatment. True prevention comes with an electron-rich alkaline lifestyle and diet. There is NO other way.

Our bodies are alkaline by design and acidic by function.

The body's basic
pH balance of
acid and alkalinity
must be
maintained.

alkaline by eating certain types of food and by eating according to our blood type. We can also become more alkaline by drinking alkaline water, such as water with lemon.

The equilibrium in the body is imperative for good health. The body's basic pH balance of acid and alkalinity must be maintained. Edgar Cayce, the sleeping prophet, was one of the first to let us know that disease cannot live in true alkalinity. He spoke of using lemon water to turn the body alkaline. He taught that when the body is alkaline, colds, flus, and mucus cannot survive. Now we know that many other diseases cannot live in alkalinity.

Small chemical
fluctuation in
any one of the
number of body
fluids or functions
may have strong
implications toward
health or illness.

Small chemical fluctuation in any one of the number of body fluids or functions may have strong implications toward health or illness. For example a certain change in only of few degrees of body heat can cause severe sickness or even death, if we don't take care of it. Similarly pH equilibrium is vitally important. Proper pH balance has been identified by biochemists and medical physiologists as a most important aspect of a balanced healthy body. A pH of 7.4 is considered desirable for the human body. A drop in blood pH level to a reading of 6.95 can lead to serious health risks, such as coma or death.

As the sayings go prevention is better than cure and you are what

you eat. The futurist and inventor Thomas Edison said over 100 years ago, "Doctors of the future will prescribe no medicines, but will prescribe food and will interest their patients in the care of the human frame, in diet and in the cause and prevention of disease."

To provide the best environment for the cells, concentrate your meals around simple, "real" food, such as raw or steamed vegetables and steamed brown rice. Fresh, organically grown fruits and veggies should be used whenever possible. Dark green and orange veggies have the highest nutritional value. Research indicates that phytochemicals from cruciferous vegetables such as broccoli, brussels sprouts, cabbage, and cauliflower, as well as turnips and kale support the detoxification processes within the body. Include these vegetables whenever possible. Be sure that your diet contains adequate protein to supply the building materials necessary for tissue repair. Soy products such as tofu and tempeh are excellent sources of vegetable protein. Soy protein is complete (containing all essential amino acids) for human needs. For animal protein, free-range or organically raised meats and poultry or wild game are our best choices. Fresh fish is also an excellent source of protein.

It is best to eat a variety of foods and rotate your selections so that you can halt any reaction to specific foods. Water is very important to help flush wastes and toxins out of our body. You should drink at least 8-10 oz glasses of purified or microwater each day. If you don't feel that you can drink that much plain water everyday, green tea or herbal teas will give you variety plus an excellent source of even more antioxidants. Avoid carbonated drinks.

Acidity – Alkalinity

What are acidity and alkalinity and how do they affect human health?

This subject is of vital importance!

Scientists report that over 150 degenerative diseases are caused by high acid levels in the body. Knowing this fact, we should begin by understanding what acidity and alkalinity are and how they relate to our health.

The pH scale ranges from 0 to 14, with 0 being extremely acidic, 14 being extremely alkaline, and 7 being neutral. Body fluids range between 4.5 and 7.5 pH (blood must maintain 7.35 to 7.45 pH). A one point drop on the pH scale is 10 times more acidic; for example from 7 to 6 is 10 times more acidic, from 7 to 5 is 100 times, from 7 to 2 is 1,000,000 times more acidic.

Most plants and fish thrive in waters of pH values from 6.6 to 7.4. This is a good rule of thumb to use for humans as parasites, viruses, bad bacteria, and degenerative diseases are more prevalent in an acidic system. In order for the body to remain healthy, it keeps a delicate and precise balance of blood pH at 7.365, which is slightly alkaline. The body does whatever it has to in order to maintain this balance. The problem is that most people have incredibly acid-forming lifestyles. Acid is produced in your body whenever you have stress, upset emotions, and when the food you eat is acid-forming.

The human body is composed of 78% water. The cells in the body are 98% water. Even our bones are 20% water. We can live for thirty days without food but only 3 days without water. If all the water is removed from a 150 pound person, the residue left would weigh less than 35 pounds. We know that the body fluids of healthy people are slightly alkaline while the same fluids of those who are sick are acidic, either very acidic or slightly. Generally speaking, the more acid your body is, the more serious the illness you have. The degree of acidity significantly affects the body's ability to prevent and/or reverse illness and disease (including such degenerative diseases as cancer, diabetes, heart disease, and others). Individuals that have severe health challenges almost invariably also

Scientists report that over 150 degenerative diseases are caused by high acid levels in the body.

Generally speaking, the more acid your body is, the more serious the illness you have.

41

have high acidity. Unfortunately, acidity has become a national epidemic that is one of the most ignored or unknown underlying causes of many of the degenerative diseases of the western world.

✓ High systemic acid levels contribute or cause directly, numerous health problems;

✓ Acid systems can't use calcium effectively.

✓ They can't maintain proper blood oxygen levels and cancer can only develop in an oxygen poor, acidic environment.

✓ Acidic blood can't circulate properly creating extra strain on the heart.

✓ It adversely affects the digestive system and the lymphatic system.

How is this condition created?

Our acid problems are due to a combination of two chronic habits:

1. What we eat and drink
2. What we are not taking in (nutrients, vitamins, minerals, water, etc.).

Whatever comes into contact with our skin, lungs, and digestive system is absorbed into the body very quickly. To achieve and maintain a healthy alkaline body, we must eat foods and drinks that produce an alkaline body.

The Standard American Diet (SAD) consists of fast food, high protein, fat, sugar, and carbohydrates which contribute to an overly acidic body. In addition, Americans eat next to no vegetables and the vegetables that are eaten are often cooked thereby creating another acidifying food whereas raw, unprocessed vegetables are alkalizing to the body. In general, it is important to eat a diet that contains both acidic and alkalizing foods. People vary, but for most the ideal diet is 75 percent alkalizing and 25 percent acidifying.

Dr. Bruce Ames, noted biochemist at the University of California at Berkeley at a 1998 conference of the Society of Toxicology, told the audience of researchers that nutrient deficiency may explain why the 25% of the population that eats the least fruit and vegetables has double the cancer rate in comparison to the 25% of the population that eats the most fruits and vegetables. — *Lack of Vitamins may cause Cancer"* Reuters, October, 28, 1998

It is probable that the population that eats higher amounts of vegetables and fruits is also more alkaline than the rest of us. It only makes sense. It isn't just the nutrient content of the food; it is the acid vs. alkaline ratios that are positively affected as well.

The National Health and Nutrition Survey reported that:

- ✓ Less than 10% of Americans consumed five daily servings of fruit and vegetables

- ✓ 40% ate no fruit or fruit juice

- ✓ 50% ate no vegetables

- ✓ 70% have no dietary vitamin C

- ✓ 80% didn't eat anything that had carotenoids

- ✓ The number one vegetable in the United States is French Fries and that comprises 25% of all vegetables eaten.

- ✓ Number two is Iceberg Lettuce and a close third is Ketchup.

If we can't even eat the minimal amount of alkalizing foods it is no wonder we have such nationwide issues with degenerative diseases caused by acidity.

Dehydration is rampant often because the average American thinks that drinking soda or coffee is the same as drinking water. As well as acting as a diuretic, soda has an acidic range around 2.5 pH. It takes an incredible amount of "good" water to counteract the effects of soda. You may have to drink nearly 32 glasses of 7.0 pH water to eliminate the bad effects of 1 glass of soda. In addition to soda, coffee, caffeine, and smoking all contribute to raising the acid levels in one's body, thereby contributing to serious health problems. It is important to understand that raising the body's pH does not cure disease. It does however, allow the body to heal itself by normalizing cellular function and ridding itself of toxins. Also fruits and vegetables will be adding the minerals that are so important to maintaining good health.

Alkalizing Diet

We need to choose a diet which is balanced on the side of alkaline-forming foods. All natural, raw, vegetable and fruit juices are alkaline-producing. Fruit juices become more acid-producing when processed and especially when sweetened. A food's acid or alkaline-forming tendency in the body has nothing to do with the actual pH of the food itself. For example, lemons are very acidic; however, the end products they produce after digestion and assimilation are very alkaline — so in fact lemons are alkaline-forming in the body.

Likewise, meat will test alkaline before digestion but it leaves very acidic residue in the body. So, like nearly all animal products, meat is very acid-forming.

A severe acid condition forces the body to borrow minerals —

It is important to understand that raising the body's pH does not cure disease. It does however, allow the body to heal itself by normalizing cellular function and ridding itself of toxins.

All natural, raw, vegetable and fruit juices are alkaline-producing.

Meat will test alkaline before digestion but it leaves very acidic residue in the body.

including calcium, sodium, potassium, and magnesium from organs and bones to buffer (neutralize) the acid to safely remove it from the body. This is a primary cause of osteoporosis. Acidic conditions can also cause such problems as:

- ✓ Cardiovascular damage, weight gain, obesity. and diabetes.

- ✓ Bladder conditions, kidney stones.

- ✓ Increased propensity for depression, acceleration of free radical damage.

- ✓ Hormonal problems, premature aging.

- ✓ Aching muscles and lactic acid buildup, osteoporosis and joint pain including arthritis.

- ✓ Low energy and chronic fatigue, slow digestion and elimination.

- ✓ Yeast/fungal overgrowth, lack of energy and fatigue.

- ✓ Lower body temperature, escalation of tendency for infection.

- ✓ Immune deficiency, loss of drive, joy, and enthusiasm.

- ✓ Easily stressed, pale complexion

- ✓ Headaches, gastritis

- ✓ Loose and painful teeth, inflamed and sensitive gums

- ✓ Mouth and stomach ulcers, cracks at the corners of the lips.

- ✓ Inflammation of the corneas and eyelids, impaired digestion and excess stomach acid.

- ✓ Nails are thin and split easily, hair looks dull, has split ends, and falls out.

- ✓ Dry skin, skin easily irritated.

- ✓ Low blood oxygen levels, leg cramps and spasms

44

The Cause of Disease

Have you ever wondered if many of the diseases raging through our society have a common cause? Many doctors, herbalists, and nutritionists believe that the explanation may come down to these simple words: **pH Imbalance.**

Acid Alkaline Imbalance

Over acidity, which can become a dangerous condition that weakens all body systems, is very common today. It gives rise to an internal environment conducive to disease, as opposed to a pH balanced environment which allows normal body function necessary for the body to resist disease. A healthy body maintains adequate alkaline reserves to meet emergency demands. When excess acids must be neutralized our alkaline reserves are depleted leaving the body in a weakened condition. A pH balanced diet, according to many experts, is a vital key to health maintenance.

The concept of acid alkaline imbalance as the cause of disease is not new. In 1933 a New York doctor named William Howard Hay published a ground-breaking book, *A New Health Era* in which he maintains that all disease is caused by **autotoxication** (or "self-poisoning") due to acid accumulation in the body:

> *Now we depart from health in just the proportion to which we have allowed our alkalies to be dissipated by introduction of acid-forming food in too great amount... It may seem strange to say that all disease is the same thing, no matter what its myriad modes of expression, but it is verily so.*
>
> —William Howard Hay, M.D.

More recently, in his remarkable book *Alkalize or Die*, Dr. Theodore A. Baroody says essentially the same thing:

> *The countless names of illnesses do not really matter. What does matter is that they all come from the same root cause...* ***too much tissue acid waste in the body!***
>
> —Theodore A. Baroody, N.D., D.C., Ph.D.

Over acidity gives rise to an internal environment conducive to disease, as opposed to a pH balanced environment which allows normal body function necessary for the body to resist disease.

45

Understanding pH

pH (potential of hydrogen) is a measure of the acidity or alkalinity of a solution. It is measured on a scale of 0 to 14 — the lower the pH the more acidic the solution, the higher the pH the more alkaline (or base) the solution. When a solution is neither acid nor alkaline it has a pH of 7 which is neutral.

pH (potential of hydrogen) is a measure of the acidity or alkalinity of a solution. It is measured on a scale of 0 to 14.

Water is the most abundant compound in the human body, comprising 70% of the body. The body has an acid-alkaline (or acid-base) ratio called the pH which is a balance between positively charged ions (acid-forming) and negatively charged ions (alkaline-forming.) The body continually strives to balance pH. When this balance is compromised many problems can occur.

It is important to understand that we are not talking about stomach acid or the pH of the stomach. We are talking about the pH of the body's fluids and tissues which is an entirely different matter.

The body continually strives to balance pH. When this balance is compromised many problems can occur.

Test Your Body's Acidity or Alkalinity with pH Strips:

It is recommended that you test your pH levels to determine if your body's pH needs immediate attention. By using pH test strips, you can determine your pH factor quickly and easily in the privacy of your own home. If your urinary pH fluctuates between 6.0 to 6.5 in the morning and between 6.5 and 7.0 in the evening, your body is functioning within a healthy range. If your saliva stays between 6.5 and 7.5 all day, your body is functioning within a healthy range. The best time to test your pH is about one hour before a meal and two hours after a meal. Test your pH two days a week.

pH and Bone Loss:

A recent seven-year study conducted at the University of California, San Francisco, on 9,000 women showed that those who have chronic acidosis are at greater risk for bone loss than those who have normal pH levels. The scientists who carried out this experiment believe that many of the hip fractures prevalent among middle-aged women are connected to high acidity caused by a diet rich in animal foods and a low in vegetables. This is because the body borrows calcium from the bones in order to balance pH.

— American Journal of Clinical Nutrition

Study of women showed that those who have chronic acidosis are at greater risk for bone loss than those who have normal pH levels.

Most people who suffer from unbalanced pH are acidic. This condition forces the body to borrow minerals — including calcium, sodium, potassium, and magnesium — from vital organs and bones to buffer (neutralize) the acid and safely remove it from the body. Because of this strain, the body can suffer severe and prolonged damage due to high acidity, a condition that may go undetected for years.

Mild acidosis can cause such problems as:

➤ Cardiovascular damage, including the constriction of blood vessels and the reduction of oxygen.

➤ Weight gain, obesity, and diabetes.

➤ Bladder and kidney conditions, including kidney stones.

➤ Immune deficiency.

➤ Acceleration of free radical damage, possibly contributing to cancerous mutations.

➤ Hormone concerns.

➤ Premature aging.

➤ Osteoporosis; weak, brittle bones, hip fractures, and bone spurs.

➤ Joint pain, aching muscles, and lactic acid buildup.

➤ Low energy and chronic fatigue.

➤ Slow digestion and elimination.

➤ Yeast/fungal overgrowth

Urine pH

Urine testing may indicate how well your body is excreting acids and assimilating minerals, especially calcium, magnesium, sodium, and potassium. These minerals function as "buffers." Buffers are substances that help maintain and balance the body against the introduction of too much acidity or too much alkalinity. Even with the proper amounts of buffers, acid or alkaline levels can become extreme.

When the body ingests or produces too many of these acids or alkalis, it must excrete the excess. The urine is the perfect way for the body to remove any excess acids or alkaline substances that cannot be buffered. If the average urine pH is below 6.5 the body's buffering system is overwhelmed, a state of "autotoxication" exists, and attention should be given to lowering acid levels.

Buffers are substances that help maintain and balance the body against the introduction of too much acidity or too much alkalinity.

Saliva pH

The results of saliva testing may indicate the activity of digestive enzymes in the body. These enzymes are primarily manufactured by the stomach, liver, and pancreas. While the saliva also utilizes buffers just like the urine, it relies on this process to a much lesser degree. If the saliva pH is too low (below 6.5), the body may be producing too many acids or may be overwhelmed by acids because it has lost the ability to adequately remove them through the urine. If the saliva pH is too high (over 6.8), the body may suffer greatly, e.g. excess gas, constipation and production of yeast, mold and fungus. Some people will have acidic pH readings from both urine and saliva—this is referred to as "double acid."

Restoring pH Balance in the Body

Your body is able to assimilate minerals and nutrients properly only when its pH is balanced. It is therefore possible for you to be taking healthy nutrients and yet be unable to absorb or use them. If you are not getting the results you expected from your nutritional or herbal program, look for an acid alkaline imbalance. Even the right herbal program may not work if your body's pH is out of balance.

If the saliva pH is too high (over 6.8), the body may suffer greatly, e.g. excess gas, constipation and production of yeast, mold and fungus.

Keeping Your Body's pH in Balance

Your body also has a pH value. In fact, all your body fluids each have a pH value. The adult body is about 60% fluid. This fluid fills every cell, the spaces between cells, and so forth. This fluid can be neutral, acidic, or basic. As far as can be determined the body functions best when these fluids are neutral which is to say neither acidic or basic. (7.0)

The blood that is a small proportion of the total body fluid is an exception being significantly more basic (7.3-7.4 pH). Don't get confused by stomach acidity or colon acidity as this is a totally different system then the internal system of the body.

Setting aside the blood and the digestive system, the internal fluids of the body (60% of the total body weight) should be neutral. When these fluids are acidic, they are irritants. If 60% of the body is irritating the other 40% there is a chronic non-optimum situation.

How does the body get acidic?

The body has natural mechanisms to eliminate acids. It can handle the natural acids created by the body which are created in energy production and the process of rebuilding cells. However, the extra acidity created by a poor diet has the body systems overwhelmed with a backlog of acids. This pH (acidity/alkaline) is important to the health of living organisms.

What are the results of too much acidity?

The Japanese feel that the degenerative diseases as osteoporosis, cancers, arthritis, etc. are primarily due to acidosis (the system being too acid).

Based on testimonials, conditions ranging from dandruff and fungus under the toe to diabetes and cancer have lessened or in some cases gone into full remission simply by achieving a proper acid/base balance.

When a body is acidic, it creates a welcoming environment for viruses and bacteria to come in and begin to flourish. As viruses and bacteria continue to flourish inside our body, we experience lack of energy, frequent illness, and pains. If a person doesn't do

When a body is acidic, it creates a welcoming environment for viruses and bacteria to come in and begin to flourish.

49

anything about changing the acidic state of the body, the situation can get worse. Virus or bacteria can mutate into a serious illness.

B acteria and viruses perish in alkaline environment because a pH balanced or alkaline body doesn't create the environment for viruses and bacteria to thrive and flourish.

Conversely, bacteria and viruses perish in alkaline environment because a pH balanced or alkaline body doesn't create the environment for viruses and bacteria to thrive and flourish. Thus, no bacteria or virus will enter an alkaline body, grow and mutate into serious illness or disease.

The bottom line is that we need to handle the reasons the body becomes acidic and there are some things that can be done. Its not only the poor nutrition, but the constant bombardment of the body by pollutants, poisons, and chemicals that we either ingest, breath, or put into our body daily...

What does the body need to balance its pH?

The acids build up in your system thus causing your body's pH to be out of balance. When this occurs, your body will restore its optimal pH by depleting certain minerals, such as potassium, calcium, and magnesium from your organs and bones. You can help your body neutralize acids in the blood and maintain a balanced pH by taking some simple steps liking eating the right foods, exercising, and lessening the amount of chemicals you put in your body.

What Causes Acidity?

The reason acidosis is more common in our society is mostly due to the typical American diet which is far too high in acid-producing animal products like meat, eggs, and dairy, and far too low in alkaline-producing foods like fresh vegetables. Additionally, we eat acid-producing processed foods like white flour and sugar and drink acid-producing beverages like coffee and soft drinks. We use too many drugs, which are acid-forming; and we use artificial chemical sweeteners like NutraSweet, Equal, or aspartame which are extremely acid-forming. One of the best things we can do to correct an overly-acid body is to clean up the diet and lifestyle.

What exactly does pH mean? pH is the short form for 'potential hydrogen.' The pH of any solution is the measure of its hydrogen-ion concentration. The higher the pH reading, the more alkaline and oxygen rich the fluid is. The lower the pH reading, the more acidic and oxygen deprived the fluid is. The pH ranges from 0 to 14, with 7.0 being neutral. Indicator above 7.0 is alkaline and below 7.0 is considered acidic.

Acidic vs Alkaline Foods

Food you eat is burned or metabolized when consumed, leaving an ash residue that is released into the blood. This ash residue can be acidic, alkaline, or neutral regardless of the original pH of the food before digestion. For example, a grapefruit is acidic undigested, but the ash residue is alkaline after it's metabolized. In general, the higher the mineral content of the food the more alkaline the ash residue is. Your body strives for a proper pH — slightly alkaline or neutral — by filtering and buffering acid residues.

Importance of pH Balance

To buffer acids, your body releases minerals from bones. Your kidneys also process and filter the acids to be removed as waste. If your kidneys are unable to filter enough acids or you have insufficient quantities of minerals to buffer acids, disease or even death can occur.

According to Dr. Mark Stengler, a naturopathic physician and author, many diseases and health conditions are associated with an over-acidic body. Stengler asserts these diseases include osteoporosis, muscle loss, kidney stones, fractures, diabetes, high blood pressure, heart disease, thyroid

The American diet is far too high in acid-producing animal products like meat, eggs and dairy, and far too low in alkaline-producing foods like fresh vegetables.

The pH of any solution is the measure of its hydrogen-ion concentration.

To buffer acids, your body releases minerals from bones. Your kidneys also process and filter the acids to be removed as waste.

51

problems, and cancer. The body functions optimally when a suitable acid to alkaline balance is maintained.

Acid-forming Foods

Most animal foods like meat, dairy, and eggs are acid-forming; beef, pork, and shellfish are highly acid-forming. With the exception of almonds and chestnuts, nuts and seeds are acid-forming. Peanuts and walnuts are very acid-forming. Grains are acid-forming, with refined grains being more acidic than whole grains. Fruits are almost evenly split with blackberries, cranberries, cherries, rhubarb, plums, and processed fruit juices forming acid residues. White sugar is acid-forming and artificial sweeteners are highly acid-forming. Tea, coffee, alcohol, and soft drinks are all acid-forming.

Alkaline-forming Foods

Almost all vegetables are alkaline-forming with asparagus, raw spinach, broccoli, and onions highly alkaline-forming. Surprisingly two citrus fruits, grapefruits and lemons, are highly alkaline-forming when metabolized. Other fruits that are alkaline-forming include grapes, pears, apples, blueberries, bananas, oranges, and peaches. The few grains listed as alkaline-forming are quinoa, amaranth, millet, buckwheat, and wild rice. Stevia, raw honey, maple syrup, and rice syrup are included in the alkaline-forming sweeteners. Herbal teas and lemon water form an alkaline ash reside when metabolized.

Maintaining Proper pH

The bulk of your diet should consist of vegetables and fruits that are alkaline-forming to maintain an optimal acid-alkaline balance. You should limit animal products, refined carbohydrates, and sugar. Salt is also acid-forming and should be limited to 1,300mg or less daily, according to Stengler.

Susan Brown and Larry Trivieri, authors of "The Acid-Alkaline Food Guide", recommend consuming 20 percent moderately to extremely acid-forming foods and 80 percent moderately to extremely alkaline-forming foods to maintain a proper balance. If you are eating slightly acid- or alkaline-forming foods the ratio is 35 to 40 percent acid-forming and 60 to 65 percent alkaline forming.

Acid vs. Alkaline in the Body

Alkaline and acidic foods, which are classified by the effect they have

> White sugar is acid-forming and artificial sweeteners are highly acid-forming. Tea, coffee, alcohol, and soft drinks are all acid-forming.

> An over-consumption of acidic foods can lead to acidosis, which is increased acid in the bloodstream.

on urine pH levels after consumption, affect the body's pH balance levels. An overconsumption of acidic foods can lead to acidosis which is increased acid in the bloodstream. However, an increase in alkaline foods is beneficial in the body and may help to prevent disease. Fruits, vegetables, and grains are examples of alkaline foods. Meat is an example of an acidic food.

The pH Scale

The pH scale goes from 0 to 14, with 0 to 7 representing acidic foods and 7.1 to 14 representing alkalizing foods. The pH balance of the human bloodstream is one of the most important biochemical balances in the human body and the body will try to maintain an alkalizing pH of 7.4 by depositing or withdrawing minerals from bones, fluids, or soft tissues.

A proper pH is required to achieve good health, improved immunity, and to stay at a healthy weight. The more unbalanced pH levels are, the more the person is likely to develop health problems or struggle with his weight. Feeling tired, lethargic, or generally unwell are symptoms of an unbalanced pH level.

The Difference Between Acidic and Alkaline

All foods are classified into two categories, alkalizing or acidifying, based on the effect the food has on urine pH after consumption. If a food increases the acidity of urine after consumption, it is classified as an acidic food. Conversely, if a food increases the alkalinity of urine after consumption, it is classified as an alkalizing food. Alkalizing foods are extremely beneficial for the body and assist in fighting or preventing degenerative diseases such as cancer, heart disease, osteoporosis, and tooth decay. On the other hand, many acidic foods are damaging to the body and may result in acidosis. Fifty to 80 percent of total dietary calories should come from alkalizing foods to prevent acidosis and maintain the body's pH balance.

Acidosis

Excessive stress and/or an acidic diet can lead to acidosis, which is increased acidity of the blood. Stress causes the endocrine system to release excess adrenaline and other hormones which can lead to acidosis. Similarly, a diet high in acidic foods such as meat and low in alkalizing foods such as fruits and vegetables can also disrupt the pH balance in the body. When the body becomes too acidic, it will remove minerals from bones, tissues, and bodily fluids in an attempt to regulate pH levels. Undetected, acidosis can

The pH balance of the human bloodstream is one of the most important biochemical balances in the human body and the body will try to maintain an alkalizing pH of 7.4 by depositing or withdrawing minerals from bones, fluids, or soft tissues.

Fifty to 80 percent of total dietary calories should come from alkalizing foods to prevent acidosis and maintain the body's pH balance.

cause severe health problems.

• Acidic Foods

Blueberries, cranberries, prunes, wheat, white bread, pasta, beef, pork, shellfish, cheese, ice cream, peanuts, walnuts, beer, alcohol, kidney beans, string beans, plums, store-bought juices, brown rice, rye bread, sprouted breads, organ meats, cold water fish, eggs, pumpkin, sesame seeds, sunflower seeds, corn oil, fatty dairy products, margarine, honey, skinless potatoes, pinto beans, navy beans, lima beans, canned fruits, white rice, oats, pecans, cashews, pistachios, coffee, wine, chicken, turkey, lamb, raw dairy, and most condiments are all acidic foods.

• Alkaline Foods

Citrus fruits, watermelons, mango, papaya, asparagus, onions, vegetable juices, parsley, spinach, broccoli, garlic, barley, olive oil, grape seed oil, dried fruits, melons, grapes, apples, pears, kiwis, okra, squash, green beans, beets, celery, lettuce, zucchini, sweet potatoes, amaranth, quinoa, millet, lentils, wild rice, corn, bananas, cherries, pineapples, peaches, avocados, carrots, tomatoes, mushrooms, cabbage, peas, cauliflower, turnips, olives, canola oil, raw sugar, coconuts, chestnuts, hazelnuts, goat cheese, whey, and soy products are all alkalizing foods.

• Nonfood Sources that Affect pH

Probiotics, commonly found in yogurts, create an acidic environment in the digestive tract. Likewise, soft water and distilled water tend to be acidic because the water has little to no minerals. On the other hand, mineral water and hard water are alkalizing because of their mineral content. Additionally, antibiotics, mineral supplements, vitamins and antacids can affect the pH of urine.

Daily poisons that bring about acidity

Have you looked at the chemicals that you put in your body? Read the labels on the processed foods we eat — aspartame, phosphorus (as in soda), caffeine (binds up calcium so it can't be used in the body). They and others create an acidic state in body.

Undetected, acidosis can cause severe health problems.

We are daily bombarding the body with poisons.

Clothing, towels, and bedding washed with this chemical retain it in the fabric. Our body's are wrapped in underwear and clothes impregnated with chemicals. When we take a bath and have open pores we dry ourselves with towels laden with chemicals. We wash dishes with these chemicals. Carpets are cleaned with chemicals, glass windows and doors, floors that baby's crawl on.

Many people exercise, follow a good diet, take nutritional supplements, control stress and do detoxification regimes, but they don't look at the chemicals that they're exposed to or using such as household cleaners, personal hygiene products, at home and in the work place.

Look at what your using and see how many products contain any of these chemicals (there are more but below are the most prevalent):

- *Sodium Lauryl Sulfate*: known to be carcinogenic — found in toothpaste, shampoo, etc.

- *Cocaminde DEA*: known to be carcinogenic to animals — found in even the "natural" soap powders because its made from coconuts?

- *Propylene Glycol*: this is in antifreeze — implicated with contact dermatitis, etc.

- *Phenol*: coal tar — causes nausea, convulsions, coma, etc.

- *Iodopropynl Butyl Carbamate*: adversely affects liver, etc.

- *Organophosphate* is an insecticide actually used to kill spider mites from agricultural fields. Farmers, their families and pets are warned to stay out of a sprayed field for a minimum of forty-eight hours. So why is this vigorous insecticide in our laundry powder?

- *Blue #1, Yellow #5, and Red #40*: all coal tar derivatives.

How do we get these chemicals into our system?

We brush our teeth with them, wash our face with them, they are found in our deodorants. They are found in hairspray, perfumes, makeup, cleansers, and moisturizers. We dry clean our clothes in them.

Even common *soap* is made from cattle and pigs (animal fats). The

We are daily bombarding the body with poisons.

Most people don't look at the chemicals that they're exposed to or using such as household cleaners, personal hygiene products, at home and in the work place.

antibiotics and hormones that are in the animal systems are then transferred into your body system. In addition, your skin also can get plugged up using these animal fats and cannot get rid of wastes through this system of detoxification — the skin.

The products with chemicals in them are very easily assimilated into the person using them. Deodorant's chemicals are very easily to absorb into the lymphatic passages and to your body's systems. Aluminum can get into the brain since it can pass the blood brain barrier — and aluminum products researchers say may cause Alzheimer's. The more "natural" deodorants have propylene glycol in them and that is a petroleum product found in many products including makeup.

What can you do to help your body's pH:

We need to use soaps and ingredients that are not full of poisons and there is product that is a powerful combination of natural ingredients that neutralize and remove toxins from the human body. It is very effective. We've used it ourselves and found our pH becoming less acid. When we first used the soap in place of regular body soap for showers, a real detox started to happen with headaches and other manifestations. That was just using the soap.

The only deodorant we've found without these poisons is the "mineral stones" that can be found in the health food stores — they last a long time as well.

Find your Body's pH

There are a variety of ways to determine your body's pH, the most accurate of which is to find the pH value of your blood using a pH meter. However, that can be impractical since it would require drawing blood and purchasing a special meter. A more practical and inexpensive method is to find the pH level of your urine using litmus paper. But, since your urine pH various with what you eat, you should measure your pH after fasting for at least 12 hours, or when you get up in the morning before you exercise, eat or drink anything.

Balancing Your Body Chemistry

You can change your shape to slim down to your ideal weight — naturally and permanently. Despite what you may believe, weight loss is not about fat grams, cholesterol, carbs, or calories. It's all about acid. According to Dr. Robert Young, renowned microbiologist and nutritionist, reaching your ideal weight is simply a matter of maintaining the delicate pH balance of the blood.

Reclaiming Your High Energy Levels

A surprising body-chemical imbalance may be to blame for stubborn fat, low energy, and frequent illness — but there are foods that can rebalance your system quickly. Learn what they are and how to consume them properly.

The Medical Profession Needs To Understand Nutrition

Too often, doctors react to illness with surgery, drugs, or radical treatment. They do not often promote prevention, especially in the form of diet change. And when diet is discussed, usually the concern is placed on weight or fat — not on acidity.

How do you know if you're overly acidic? Fat is an Acid Problem!

Perhaps one of Dr. Young's most well known discoveries is his theory of the cause of overweight. He has shown that fat is actually an over-acidification problem. What does that mean? The body creates fat cells to carry acids away from your vital organs, so these acids literally don't choke your organs to death. Fat is saving your life! Fat is actually a response from the body to an alarming over-acidic condition. The solution? Alkalize and energize.

What about Underweight?

At the other end of the health spectrum, the yeast and fungus produced within an overly acidic body can feed on your nutrients and reduce the chemical and mechanical absorption of everything you eat by as much as 50%. This causes many people to become excessively thin, which is no healthier than becoming overweight. Without protein, your body cannot rebuild new tissues or produce enzymes, hormones, or hundreds of other chemical components necessary for cell energy and organ activity. Fatigue, illness,

Despite what you may believe, weight loss is not about fat grams, cholesterol, carbs, or calories. It's all about acid.

The body creates fat cells to carry acids away from your vital organs, so these acids literally don't choke your organs to death. Fat is saving your life!

and body weight changes are the results. An underweight person may loose a little more weight as their body chemistry stabilizes. As their body normalizes, they will begin to gain towards their ideal weight.

Healthy bodies are not overweight or underweight. A healthy body naturally maintains its own ideal weight. You can begin to restore health, balance, and harmony to your body with *Dr. Young's Complete Program*. As alkalizing and oxygenation begins to take place, the body naturally begins to seek its own ideal weight.

Allergies

The toxins produced within an overly acidic, oxygen deprived body may contribute significantly to what are often called the symptoms of allergy. In addition, the absorption of undigested proteins is a major cause of allergy conditions. The digestive system is weakened, which prevents the total breakdown of amino acids often causing food allergies. This alone may produce a wide spectrum of severe allergic reactions.

Fatigue

Fatigue is probably the major symptom or complaint of an overly acidic body. The toxins produced in an acidic body environment reduce the absorption of protein and minerals, which in turn weakens the body's ability to produce enzymes and hormones. This also interferes with the reconstruction of cells and other necessary components of energy production. The result is fatigue, poor endurance, an inability to add muscle tone, and general weakness.

The Importance of an Alkaline Environment

Forget cholesterol counts. Forget calories and fat grams. Forget blood pressure, blood sugar, hormone levels, or any of the other markers of health you're used to at the doctor's office. It turns out that the single measurement most important to your health is the pH of your blood and tissues — how acidic or alkaline it is. Different areas of the body have different ideal pH levels, but blood pH is the most telling of all. Just as your body temperature is rigidly regulated, the blood must be kept in a very narrow pH range — mildly basic or alkaline. The body will go to great lengths to preserve that, including wreaking havoc on other tissues or systems.

The pH level of our internal fluids affects every cell in our bodies. The entire metabolic process depends on an alkaline environment. Chronic over acidity corrodes body tissue and if left unchecked will interrupt all cellular activities and functions, from the beating of your heart to the neutral firing of your brain. In other words, over-acidity interferes with life itself. It is at the root of all sickness and disease.

If that's not enough to get you interested in balancing your body pH naturally, nondestructively, keep this mind: **Over-acidity is also what's keeping you <u>FAT</u>!**

The goal then is to create the proper alkaline balance within your body. The way to do that is by eating the proper balance of alkaline and acid foods. That means 80 percent of your diet must be alkalizing foods, like green vegetables. (That percentage will go down somewhat once you've successfully rebalanced yourself.) In addition, high quality supplements will help you achieve and maintain pH balance.

Because one of the BIGGEST concerns that people have is weight loss, please go onto the next article and let's talk about that subject next.

Overacidity is Keeping You <u>FAT!</u>

Many Americans view a healthy lifestyle as something difficult to attain — and something that's not much fun. Traditional diets have taught us that to lose weight, we must count calories, keep track of everything we eat, and deprive ourselves by limiting the amount, and kinds, of foods we eat. Diets tell us exactly what and how much food to eat, regardless of our preferences and individual relationships with hunger and satiety. Dieting can help us lose weight (fat, muscle, and water) in the short term but is so unnatural and so unrealistic that it can never become a lifestyle that we can live with, let alone enjoy!

While very few diets teach healthy low-fat shopping, cooking, and dining-out strategies, many offer unrealistic recommendations and encourage health-threatening restrictions. Even more important, diets don't teach us the safest, most effective ways to exercise; they don't teach us how to deal with our cravings and our desires, or how to attend to our feelings of hunger and fullness. Eventually, we become tired of the complexity, the hunger, the lack of flavor, the lack of flexibility, the lack of energy, and the feeling of deprivation. We quit our diets and gain back the weight we've lost; sometimes we gain even more!

Each time we go on another diet of deprivation, the weight becomes more difficult to lose, and we become even more frustrated and discouraged. Then we eat more and exercise less, causing ourselves more frustration, discouragement, and depression. Soon we are in a vicious cycle. We begin to ask ourselves, "Why bother?" We begin to blame ourselves for having no will power when what we really need is clear, scientifically-based information that will help us develop a healthier lifestyle we can live with for the rest of our lives.

Deliberate restriction of food intake in order to lose weight or to prevent weight gain, known as dieting, is the path that millions of people all over the world are taking in order to reach a desired body weight or appearance. Preoccupation with body shape, size, and weight creates an unhealthy lifestyle of emotional and physical deprivation. Diets take control away from us.

Many of us who diet get caught

Dieting can help us lose weight (fat, muscle, and water) in the short term but is so unnatural and so unrealistic that it can never become a lifestyle that we can live with, let alone enjoy!

Rather than making us feel better about ourselves, diets set us up for failure and erode our self-esteem.

Most diets are too drastic to maintain; they are unrealistic and unpleasant; they are physically and emotionally stressful.

Only 5 percent of people who go on diets are successful. Please understand that we are not failing diets; diets are failing us.

in a "yo-yo" cycle that begins with low self-acceptance and results in structured eating and living because we lack trust in our body and are unwilling to listen and adhere to our body's signals of hunger and fullness. On diets, we distrust and ignore internal signs of appetite, hunger, and our need to be physically and psychologically satisfied. Instead, we depend on diet plans, measured portions, and a prescribed frequency for eating.

As a result, many of us have lost the ability to eat in response to our physical needs; we experience feelings of deprivation, then binge, and finally terminate our "health" program. This in turn leads to guilt, defeat, weight gain, low self-esteem, and then we're back to the beginning of the yo-yo diet cycle. Rather than making us feel better about ourselves, diets set us up for failure and erode our self-esteem.

The attitudes and practices acquired through years of dieting are likely to result in a body weight and size obsession, low self-esteem, poor nutrition and excessive or inadequate exercise. Weight loss from following a rigid diet is usually temporary. Most diets are too drastic to maintain; they are unrealistic and unpleasant; they are physically and emotionally stressful. And most of us just resume our old eating and activity patterns. Diets control us; we are not in control. People who try to live by diet lists and rules learn little or nothing about proper nutrition and how to enjoy their meals, physical activity, and a healthy lifestyle. No one can realistically live in the diet mode for the rest of their life, depriving themselves of the true pleasures of healthy eating and activity.

We Don't Fail Diets... They Fail Us!

Decades of research have shown that diets, both self-initiated and professionally-led, are ineffective at producing long-term health and weight loss (or weight control). When your diet fails to keep the weight off, you may say to yourself, "If only I didn't love food so much... If I could just exercise more often... If I just had more will power." The problem is not personal weakness or lack of will power. Only 5 percent of people who go on diets are successful. Please understand that we are not failing diets; diets are failing us.

The reason 95 percent of all traditional diets fail is simple. When you go on a low-calorie diet, your body thinks you are starving; it actually becomes more efficient at storing fat by slowing down your metabolism. When you stop this unrealistic eating plan, your metabolism is still slow and inefficient so that you gain the weight back even faster, even though you may still be eating less than you were before you went on the diet.

In addition, low-calorie diets cause you to lose both muscle and fat in equal amounts. However, when you eventually gain back the weight, it is all fat and not muscle, causing your metabolism to slow down even more. Now you have extra weight, a less healthy body composition, and a less attractive physique.

Diets require you to sacrifice by being hungry; they don't allow you to enjoy the foods you love. This does not teach you habits which you can maintain after the diet is over. Most diet programs force you to lower your caloric intake to dangerously low levels. The common theory is that if you eat fewer calories than you burn, you will lose weight. But when you eat fewer calories than your body needs to maintain its life-sustaining activities, you're actually losing muscle in addition to fat. Your body breaks down its own muscles to provide the needed energy for survival.

Traditional diets which use calorie restriction to produce weight loss are no longer appropriate. Most weight-loss programs measure success solely in terms of the number of pounds lost per weight loss attempt. Diets don't take into account the quality of the process used to achieve that weight loss or

the very small likelihood of sustained weight loss. For long-term good health, you need to move away from low-calorie diets and focus on enjoyable physical activity and good nutrition. Exercising regularly and eating lean-supporting calories, protein and complex carbohydrates, and reducing fat-supporting acidic calories will not only help you look and feel better, it will also significantly reduce your risk of disease.

America spends billions of dollars on different ways to fix people. If we focused more on prevention and on improving our day-to-day behaviors, we could cut health care costs in half. Contrary to popular belief, leading a healthy lifestyle doesn't have to be difficult; it doesn't have to painful or time-consuming. Making gradual, simple changes in your diet and physical activity will make great improvements in your health and well-being, and they can drastically reduce your risk of disease.

If your weight management program is to be a success, everything you eat and every exercise you do must be a pleasurable experience. If you're not enjoying yourself, it is unlikely that you'll continue your program. It's that simple. These small, gradual changes are not painful or overwhelming, but rather the core of an exciting lifestyle that you will

Low-calorie diets cause you to lose both muscle and fat in equal amounts.

For long-term good health, you need to move away from low-calorie diets and focus on enjoyable physical activity and good nutrition.

Eating high-alkaline foods help maintain the acid/base balance of your system.

look forward to.

Take the frustration, guilt, and deprivation out of weight management and allow yourself to adopt gradual, realistic changes into your life that will make healthy eating and physical activity a permanent pleasure. You will soon discover what your body is capable of and begin to look, act, and feel your very best. Good luck and enjoy all the wonderful benefits of a healthy, active lifestyle.

Every Man Needs A Good W.O.M.A.N. In Fact, Every Woman Needs A Good W.O.M.A.N.

Simply stated, in order to maintain the cycle of balance within your system, everyone needs a good W.O.M.A.N. The acronym stands for:

(W)ater: Hydration is essential. Drink lots and lots of **water** — at least one gallon per day.

(O)xygen: Cells need **oxygen** to produce energy.

(M)inerals: The body uses **minerals** to perform many different functions from building strong bones to transmitting nerve impulses.

(A)lkalinity: Eating **high-alkaline** foods help maintain the acid/base balance of your system.

(N)utrients: The seven **nutrient** groups are — proteins, carbohydrates, fats, vitamins, minerals, roughage, and fluid.

The Imbalance of the Blood

Just as our body temperature must be maintained at 98.6 degrees Fahrenheit, our blood is ideally maintained at 7.365 pH — very mildly basic. You can also measure the pH of the urine and saliva, but the blood is the most important and needs to stay within the tightest range.

Different areas of the body have different pH requirements anyway. For example, the blood and tissues should be slightly basic, but the lower bowel should be slightly acidic, and the urine should be slightly acidic or neutral. Saliva tends to be erratic. The pH of urine can provide the best estimate of what's happening in the body's tissues, but it is not always accurate. Blood pH is more reliable and thus a better indicator of internal conditions.

Physiological disease is almost always the result of too much acid stressing the body's pH balance, to the point where it provokes the body into producing symptoms of disease. (Disease can also be simply the toxic effects of an external source, but that is much more rare.)

Symptoms can be the expression of that stress, but they can also be a sign of the body's effort to balance it. Depending on the level and extent of the stress, symptoms may or may not be obviously noticeable. The kicker is that excess acid is something we do to ourselves, thanks to the choices we make. The good news, then, is that once we recognize that fact, we can make different choices.

All the body's regulatory mechanisms (including breathing, circulation, digestion, and hormone production) work to balance the delicate internal acid/base balance. Our bodies cannot tolerate extended acid imbalances. In the early stages of the imbalance, the symptoms may not be very intense and include such things as skin eruptions, headaches, allergies, colds, flu, and sinus problems.

As things get further out of whack, more serious situations arise. Weakened organs and systems start to give way, resulting in dysfunctional thyroid glands, adrenals, liver, and so on. If tissue pH deviates too far to the acid side, oxygen levels decrease and cellular metabolism will stop. In other words, cells die. You die.

So, a declining pH just can't be allowed. To prevent it, when faced with

Physiological disease is almost always the result of too much acid stressing the body's pH balance, to the point where it provokes the body into producing symptoms of disease.

Excess acid is something we do to ourselves, thanks to the choices we make.

a lot of incoming acid, the blood begins to pull alkaline minerals out of our tissues to compensate. There is a family of minerals particularly suited to neutralizing or detoxifying strong acids, including sodium, potassium, calcium, and magnesium. When these minerals react with acids, they create much less detrimental substances, which are then eliminated by the body.

Now, a healthy body maintains a reserve supply of these alkaline minerals to meet emergency demands. But if there are insufficient amounts in the diet or in the reserves, they are recruited elsewhere and may be leached from the bone (as with calcium) or muscle (magnesium) where they are, of course, *needed*. This can easily lead to deficiencies — and the many and varied symptoms that come with them.

That's just the tip of the iceberg. If the acid overload gets too great for the blood to balance, excess acid is dumped into the tissues for storage. Then the lymphatic (immune) system must neutralize what it can and try to get rid of everything else. Unfortunately, "getting rid of" acid from the tissues turns out to mean dumping it right back into the blood, creating a vicious cycle of drawing out still more basic minerals from their ordinary functions and stressing the liver and kidneys besides.

Furthermore, if the lymphatic system is overloaded or it's vessels not functioning properly (a condition often caused by lack of exercise), acid builds up in the tissues.

This imbalance in the blood pH leads to irritation and inflammation and sets the stage for sickness. Acute or recurrent illnesses result from either the body trying to mobilize mineral reserves to prevent cellular breakdown or emergency attempts to detoxify the body.

For example, the body may throw off acids through the skin, producing symptoms such as eczema, acne, boils, headaches, muscle cramps, soreness, swelling, irritation, inflammation, and general aches and pains. Chronic symptoms show up when all possibilities of neutralizing or eliminating acids have been exhausted.

When acid wastes build up in the body and enter the bloodstream, the circulatory system will try to get rid of them in liquid form, through the lungs and kidneys. If there is too much waste to handle, they are deposited in various organ systems, including the heart, pancreas, liver, and colon, or stored in fatty tissue, including the breasts, hips, thighs, belly, and and brain. This process of acid waste breakdown and disposal could also be called "the aging process."

When faced with a lot of incoming acid, the blood begins to pull alkaline minerals out of our tissues to compensate.

Chronic symptoms show up when all possibilities of neutralizing or eliminating acids have been exhausted.

This process of acid waste breakdown and disposal could also be called "the aging process."

12 Steps to Balancing pH with Food

1. **End the "breakfast food" myth. Don't let the first meal of your day slow you down!**

   Most foods and beverages people choose for the first meal of the day promote high levels of acidity, yeast, and fungi growth in the body. Foods like breakfast cereals, sweet rolls, toast, pancakes, waffles, muffins, oatmeal, maple syrup, honey, coffee, orange juice, etc., contain huge amounts of sugars and simple carbohydrates which over-acidify the blood and tissues. As you over-acidify the blood and tissues, you create a terrain that promotes the growth of bacteria, yeast, and fungi — the great decomposers of cells and tissues in the human body. What a way to start the day!

   Traditional high-protein breakfast foods like eggs, sausage, bacon, omelets, etc., also compromise the terrain and ultimately promote the growth of yeast and fungi. In addition, all meats, especially pork, are high in parasite activity.

   Therefore, when you make a commitment to balance your eating habits and improve your health, breakfast — and every meal of the day — must take on a whole new look. When you start your day, your choices for breakfast would also work well for lunch or even dinner. Any food you choose to begin the day should be good for your body any time of the day. For example: try soups for breakfast — vegetable and lentil. Other cultures like the Japanese have long served soup for breakfast, instead of the very sugary continental American and European breakfasts.

   A favorite breakfast for many people new to the alkalizing diet is millet or brown basmati rice with fresh avocado and tomato slices, soaked almonds, sunflower sprouts and flax oil. An excellent way to start the day! Vegetable soups in the morning offer a low carbohydrate, high fiber, and delicious way to start your day. Blood sugar levels are not sent soaring, causing an increase in blood insulin and a burden on your pancreas.

2. **Add liberal amounts of dark green and yellow vegetables and grasses from a wide variety of sources.**

   Fresh vegetables and grasses are an excellent source of the

Most foods and beverages people choose for the first meal of the day promote high levels of acidity, yeast, and fungi growth in the body.

Vegetable soups and in the morning offer a low carbohydrate, high fiber, and delicious way to start your day.

alkaline salts that are anti-yeast, anti-fungal, and anti-mycotoxic. The chlorophyll (or "blood of the plant") contained in plants and grasses are identical to the blood of humans, except for one atom. Green foods such as wheat grass and barley grass are some of the lowest-calorie, lowest-sugar, and most nutrient-rich foods on the planet.

> Juiced, green vegetables are very cleansing. Vegetables and grasses are also loaded with fiber.

Juiced, green vegetables are very cleansing. Vegetables and grasses are also loaded with fiber. While fruit is a good source of fiber, the high sugar content (fructose) of fruit stimulates yeast and fungal growth. Basic rule of thumb: vegetables for breakfast, vegetables for lunch, vegetables for dinner.

3. Feature in your diet low carbohydrate vegetables, legumes, and some grains.

Complex carbohydrates are highly acid forming in the body and should not exceed 20% of the diet, so eat them in moderation. Good low carbohydrate vegetables include asparagus, beets, broccoli, Brussel sprouts, cabbage, carrots, cauliflower, celery, cucumbers, eggplant, green beans, green peppers, spinach, kale, lettuce, okra, onions, garlic, parsley, radishes, and squash. Red new potatoes are the best choice in the potato family and should be used sparingly.

> Some of the best foods to eat are sprouts. Sprouted seeds become more alkaline as they grow.

Enjoy eating fresh legumes.

Stored beans can become moldy and contain mycotoxins.

Avoid stored grains. They are full of fungus-producing mycotoxins. Eat fresh — preferably sprouted — organic grains in moderation, as they are acid forming. Some of the ancient grains like amaranth, spelt, quinoa, buckwheat, and millet are more alkaline grain choices.

4. Eat lots of sprouts.

Some of the best foods to eat are sprouts. Sprouted seeds become more alkaline as they grow. They are live plant foods that are biogenic, which means they transfer their life energy to us. Sprouts can easily be grown in your kitchen during any season.

5. Increase alkali-forming foods, eat less acid-forming foods.

Good alkali forming foods include fresh sprouts, spinach, kale, Swiss chard, avocados, lemons, limes, cucumbers, celery, cauliflower, Brussel sprouts, asparagus, green beans, eggplant, broccoli, fresh tomatoes, zucchini, green/red/yellow peppers, onions, okra, garlic, parsley, watercress, cabbage, squashes, soy beans (tofu), garbanzo beans, raw almonds, Brazil nuts, hazel nuts, sesame seeds, flax seed, sprouted grains and legumes.

Green juices from all green vegetables and their tops are highly alkaline. Also, vegetable broths are extremely alkalizing to the body. These need to be yeast-free and preservative free.

Acid-forming foods you should avoid are all animal products, which include meat and milk products, refined grains and yeast products, and most fruits. These include pork, veal, most fish, beef, organ meats, chicken, turkey, eggs, shrimp, lobster, oysters, hot dogs, corned beef, pastrami, pepperoni, rice, potatoes, pasta, breads, cheeses, milk, buttermilk, sour cream, yogurt, ice cream, butter, margarine, mushrooms of all kinds, algae, corn and all corn products, coffee, tea, wine, beer, soda pop, cider, yeast products, soy sauce, ketchup, mayonnaise, vinegar, Tempe, sugar, artificial sweeteners, and of course, no candy, gum, pies, cakes, donuts, and chocolate — just to name a few.

6. Feature proteins such as broccoli, spinach, sprouts, garbanzo beans, tofu, or, fresh fish with scales and fins.

Vegetables carry the sub-cellular units and the amino acids to make proteins in amounts that are congruent with the body's needs. Also, all green vegetables are high in calcium.

What about protein? Animal protein foods provide more protein than is required by the human body. Our bodies are only 7% protein. In contrast to cow's milk which is protein rich, human mother's milk is only 5% protein (i.e., better suited to the body's protein requirements). In addition, animal protein foods often contribute factors to the body, which are unneeded and then represent a challenge to dispose of (e.g., saturated fats).

7. Drink plenty of alkaline water.

Ideally one will drink one gallon (4 liters) or more of good, structured water each day. Distilled or reverse-osmosis (purified) water are more neutral and need be brought into the alkaline range

8. Eliminate bakers or brewers yeast and all yeast-containing foods.

You should especially avoid baked goods such as bread, muffins, pies, cakes, and pastries. In America, one out of nine women will develop breast cancer. The Japanese have a much lower rate of this form of cancer and research links it with the ingestion of baked goods with bakers or brewers yeast. Research also clearly links diets with yeasty or fermented breads to gall and kidney stones and arthritis.

9. Eliminate milk, ice cream, and especially cheese.

Acid-forming foods you should avoid are all animal products which include meat and milk products, refined grains and yeast products, and most fruits.

69

There are approximately 12 grams of lactose in every eight ounces of milk that can break down into sugars that can feed yeast and fungus.

We need to understand that calcium can be pulled from the bones to help neutralize an over-acid condition which is caused when animal products are eaten.

These should not be eaten because of their lactose (milk sugar) content as well as the presence of yeast and fungus, molds, and mycotoxins. There are approximately 12 grams of lactose in every eight ounces of milk that can break down into sugars that can feed yeast and fungus. Because of the high sugar and fat content of dairy products, the fact that diary cows are fed stored grains and fungal-based antibiotics, and the fermentation process of cheese and yogurt, all diary products should be eventually eliminated from the diet. Some alternatives are soy, almond, or rice milk.

What about calcium? If milk products are eliminated, where should one turn for their calcium needs? Many worry that eating an alkaline diet would seriously deplete one's calcium intake, which is vital for so many functions of the body. All leafy, green vegetables and grasses are inherently high in calcium. We also need to understand that calcium can be pulled from the bones to help neutralize an over-acid condition which is caused when animal products are eaten; thus we see that people are suffering from a calcium-robbing problem rather than a calcium deficiency problem. As long as we are eating an alkalizing diet that is rich in green foods and green drinks, we don't need to worry about getting enough calcium.

10. Avoid fungus foods.

Mushrooms of all kinds, morels, algae, and truffles are all acid-forming foods. They contain mycotoxins which poison human cells and lead to degenerate diseases. Mushrooms in all forms are extremely poisonous whether eaten whole or in teas. There is no such thing as a good mushroom. The mushroom is not a vegetable, but rather the fruiting body of a yeast or fungus.

11. Avoid alcoholic beverages.

Wines of all kinds, beers, whiskey, brandy, gin, rum, and vodka are purely mycotoxic. Alcohol is a fungus-produced mycotoxin made by yeast, which causes direct injury to human health.

12. Avoid smoking or chewing tobacco.

It is widely understood that smoking or chewing tobacco causes cancer, but we've never understood the process — until now. Our research clearly reveals the pathway that the fermentation of the tobacco creates with yeast and sugar. Tobacco leaves are coated with yeast, fungus, and mycotoxins, which poison the cells and tissues of the body. When using tobacco, you are directly introducing dried fungus and wastes into your body.

What Acidosis Means in Terms of Health

This article is about acidity and what this means in terms of health. In short, it means that your cells are not using oxygen efficiently. In other words, instead of oxidizing they ferment and as with any ferments, acids accumulate as a by-product. This sets up a vicious cycle as an acidic cell repels oxygen and so perpetuates the problem. A fermentative environment is an unhealthy environment that supports cancer, fungal conditions such as systemic candida, and excites inflammation. It will also bring about calcium deposition in the arteries, joints, and soft tissues.

> When one is acidic it means that your cells are not using oxygen efficiently

The anomaly is that our natural metabolism produces vast amounts of acids — to be precise 10.4 mmols /minute which is 6,500 times the amount held in the body at pH 7.4. The pH (measure of acidity) has to be maintained within a very narrow range so we need to eliminate these acids as soon as they are produced. This is where breathing comes in. Breathing keeps in step with acid production — the more acid you produce (the faster the metabolism), the faster you breath. The acid is "blown off." If we stopped breathing for just 4 minutes then we would see a drop to pH 3.0 and we would die.

> Breathing keeps in step with acid production — the more acid you produce (the faster the metabolism), the faster you breath.

What goes wrong?

To understand acid production we have to look at energy production within the cell. If we follow the journey of glucose (a chief source of energy) we see that it is shuttled down a conveyor belt where each worker (enzyme) on the line modifies the glucose step-by-step to ultimately capture its energy. The waste product is carbonic acid which is split into carbon dioxide and water and easily eliminated. Problems occur when one or another worker goes on strike because he doesn't have the tools to do his job.

Our enzymes require minerals and vitamins (tools) in order to function (for example, the energy cycle enzymes require potassium, magnesium, manganese, copper, iron, B1, 2, 3, 5 and 6, CoQ10) and usually there is no problem as the food we eat comes with these very nutrients required for their metabolism. However, most of the foods consumed today are depleted of nutrients and come empty-handed.

It's a bit like ordering a construction kit. When it arrives you find that the basic materials may be present, but all the tools are missing. Without the tools you can't assemble the kit. In the body, we can go to the tool shed (bones) where we can draw on our reserves, but eventually these will also become depleted. So the workers (enzymes) become redundant and the cell accumulates partially metabolized by-products of glucose — all of which are acids.

These acids can't be broken down to carbon dioxide and water (and eliminated through the breath), but have to be neutralized or buffered within the cell until the kidneys remove them.

These acids can't be broken down to carbon dioxide and water (and eliminated through the breath), but have to be neutralized or buffered within the cell until the kidneys remove them. However, this is a much slower process and over a period of time acids will accumulate. As you can imagine, the buffering system within the cells becomes taxed. Buffers are like patrol men which capture and bind free hydrogen ions. Free hydrogen ions (H) are the measure of acidity — this is what the "H" stands for in pH. When there are no more buffers, the bones are called upon to grab the hydrogen ions.

In order for this to happen, they have to release calcium in exchange for hydrogen, and you guessed it — the bones become eroded while the soft tissues harden. So the effects of acidity are measured not so much by the overall pH of the body but by the general hardening and erosion within the system.

How do our dietary choices contribute to acidity?

High acidity arises when our nutrient intake (minerals and vitamins) fails to meet our requirements for energy production. This is when the enzymes go on strike. There are a variety of situations which exacerbate this:

- A diet high in empty foods will draw upon our nutrient reserves for its metabolism.

- Refined and processed foods where nutrients have been lost due to the refining process or damaged through processing. Refined cereals (white rice, white flour) and sugar are among the major culprits.

- A high fat diet. Fats are refined and devoid of many of the nutrients found in the whole grain or seed. Fats are nutritionally expensive requiring many nutrients for their metabolism.

- Diuretics such as caffeine and alcohol will "wash" away nutrients through the kidneys. Increased energy requirements mean increased nutrient requirements.

- Stress and stimulants (caffeine, nicotine, alcohol, recreational drugs, sugar) all stimulate energy production without supplying the raw materials or nutrients. In short, they make the body eat itself and draw on its own nutrient reserve to accomplish this.

- Fasting or skipping meals has a similar effect of inducing body breakdown and nutrient loss.

Exercise increases nutrient requirements especially for zinc, magnesium and the B vitamins. Heavy exercise regimes will deplete all nutrients unless supplied by the diet. Adolescents are the most vulnerable group as demands for zinc are high for physical and sexual maturation. Zinc deficiencies lead to mental, emotional, and physical imbalances. Certain fuels, such as protein and fat, are regarded as dirty fuels. Carbohydrate is a clean combustion fuel leaving no acidity in the tissues but protein leaves sulphuric acid and fat generally contributes to generalized acidity when taken to excess.

> **Heavy exercise regimes will deplete all nutrients unless supplied by the diet.**

There is a saying "Fat burns in the flame of carbohydrate" meaning that without some carbohydrate to stimulate the energy production line, fatty acids (from fat) will accumulate within the system. It takes up to seven days for the kidneys to remove this type of acidity, so on a high protein, high fat diet, we see a cumulative acidic effect over many years.

> **Carbohydrate is a clean combustion fuel leaving no acidity in the tissues.**

What can we do?

Make sure that your diet is unrefined, unprocessed, organic, and of high nutrient value.

Try not to take foods or drinks that will draw on your nutrient reserves.

Ensure that you have the broadest range of foods possible.

Vegetarians will need to guard against iron, zinc, vitamin D, A and B12 deficiencies.

To reduce acidity adopt a high alkaline diet (high in organic fruit and vegetables, low in fats and protein). These foods, when metabolized within the cell leave an alkaline ash. This relieves the burden on the cells' existing buffering system and will neutralize the accumulated acidity. Once this happens the electrical potential of the cell becomes more negative and oxygen (which is attracted to the negative) is drawn into the cell. Additionally, the high amount of potassium in the fruit and vegetables ousts sodium, toxins, and excess water from the cell and the cell is purged of impurities.

Remove salt (sodium chloride) from the diet. Salt increases acidic conditions and competes with potassium. Supplementation with nutrients may be applicable for deficiency states and may work in the short-term. But the solution is not this easy as an acidic cell will not readily take up nutrients and therefore long-term improvement may be difficult to achieve. However, by following the alkaline diet we can reverse acidity, improve oxidation, and enable vitamin and mineral access to the cell.

Salt increases acidic conditions and competes with potassium.

The Most Important Health Factor

To most of you, you have lived your entire lives and have never been made aware that your single most important health factor is the pH level in your blood.

The vital importance of your body's pH balance is the most unknown and overlooked issue regarding your health and your ability to live to your genetic potential!

The basic American/Western diet (meats, processed foods, white flour, sugar, alcohol, etc.) and lifestyle (and most recently the Atkins-like low-carb diets) creates a toxic, acidic state in your body. And if you drink coffee or sodas you're guaranteed to have a disease causing acidic pH. The most obvious symptoms that are seen everyday are bad breath and intestinal gas. But, the most dangerous and even deadly results of an acid blood pH are the degenerative diseases that creep up on you daily until you are suffering from the pain and agony of a heart attack, some form of cancer, or debilitating disease. Your body simply will not work to its optimum potential if it does not have a slightly alkaline pH level. You must have a slightly alkaline pH!

The startling truth is that if your body pH level is even slightly acid, you will never achieve all the health you are capable of. And worse, your body will never properly absorb the nutritional supplements you take, and will also be the breeding ground for degenerative disease".

Unfortunately, most people have an acid body pH (and you wonder why there are so many illnesses, diseases and health problems!).

The First Step in Health

If you don't feel good, don't look as good as you know you should, or have very little energy, one of the most essential things that stands between you and perfect health and remaining young, is your body's pH. To remain healthy and youthful, the first thing you must do is establish that your body's pH is properly balanced.

Proper cellular pH balance is absolutely vital for regenerating, healing, and rebuilding your body, as well as detoxifying and eliminating the accumulated toxins from the body, especially the liver and kidneys.

Your single most important health factor is the pH level in your blood.

To remain healthy and youthful, the first thing you must do is establish that your body's pH is properly balanced.

Reasons to Avoid Acidosis

We are alkaline bodies by design, but acid generating by function. Acid is produced by the parietal cells of the stomach to aid in digestion, and acid is consumed in organic form in fruit. However, other than the stomach, no part of the body should be acid.

Despite this, one of the most widespread and insidious causes of illness that plague our society is acidosis — an accumulation of more acid than the body can effectively process. Patients often initially consult a doctor seeking relief from symptoms of a chronic condition: arthritis, diabetes, emphysema, arteriosclerosis, or cancer. Regardless of the particular symptomatology, all of these conditions originate with an increase in the amount of acid in the body.

Acidosis is generally seen by medical science as a part of the pathology of several different diseases including impaired liver function. It is encountered often enough to be assumed to be normal, however, acidosis is definitely not normal. It is the forerunner of most, if not all, chronic degenerative diseases including cancer, diabetes, arthritis, and heart disease. These diseases are rampant enough to be considered epidemic in our country.

Acidosis is often a covert condition in that the patient feels good in the early stages of acid accumulation. In fact, he may boast of an exaggerated feeling of well-being and an unusually high level of energy. Unfortunately, this is an inaccurate perception resulting from the "stimulatory" reaction of the body's regulatory systems that are operating in high gear to process the excess acid. Both the good feeling and high energy level will disappear as more acid accumulates. In a continued effort to maintain alkalinity, the neutralizing alkaline reserves are depleted and the liver becomes increasingly congested and is unable to perform its function of detoxification. When the extra cellular and intracellular fluids lose their alkalinity, the person is considered to be in a condition of acidosis.

ATTITUDE AND ACIDOSIS

Prolonged periods of acidosis affect not only the physical condition but also the mental and emotional states of patients. Similarly, mental attitude can affect the physical state. It is possible for a person to maintain a diet high in fruits and vegetables and still be acid. Regardless of the diet followed, the

> Other than the stomach, no part of the body should be acid.

> Acidosis is the forerunner of most, if not all, chronic degenerative diseases including cancer, diabetes, arthritis, and heart disease.

person who is negative in his outlook on life is acid.

Negative thoughts act to stimulate the action of the adrenal glands that in turn speed up the body's metabolic activity. As this occurs, more acid is produced and since the process is continuous, the amount of acid overpowers the alkaline from the good food and the net result is acid. And the cycle can be perpetuated; the more acid we become, the more negative, defensive, argumentative and unpleasant we become. The pessimist who can find nothing good about anything is almost certainly in some degree of acidosis.

SYMPTOMS OF ACIDOSIS

Symptoms of prolonged acidosis that are caused by the consumption of excess protein can easily be mistaken for individual character or personality traits. However, definite attitudes and mannerisms develop as a result of the super-charged internal activity of the body as it works toward ridding itself of the damaging excess acid. The person who is on a high-protein diet moves through a progression of symptoms.

Initially, he...

- ✓ Has an exaggerated sense of well-being.
- ✓ Is a high achiever, a "mover and shaker".
- ✓ Believes himself to be perfectly well.
- ✓ Is overly ambitious and restless due to the irritation of the nerves.

Later he...

- ✓ Sees only the pessimistic side of issues and life.
- ✓ Can't sleep restfully.
- ✓ Wakes up as tired in the morning as he was when he went to bed.
- ✓ Constantly finds fault with everyone and everything.
- ✓ Is tired and experiences generalized aches and pains.
- ✓ Becomes irritable, ill tempered, and difficult to please.
- ✓ Shows signs of "aging" as the body removes alkalizing substances from the muscles then calcium from the bones.

Although everyone who is suffering from acidosis does not experience all of these symptoms, it is helpful for the practitioner to be able to correlate some "personality traits" with clinical findings and to recognize indications that the patient's body is over taxed and headed toward chronic degenerative disease.

10 Reasons To Avoid Acidosis

1. Corrodes Arteries, Veins, and Heart Tissues.

Like acid eating into marble, acidosis erodes and eats into cell wall membranes of the heart, arteries, and veins, weakening cardiovascular structures and inter connective tissues.

2. Accelerates Free-Radical Damage and Premature Aging.

Acidosis causes partial lipid breakdown and destructive oxidative cascades. This accelerates Free Radical Damage of cell walls and intracellular membrane structures, which then unravel, killing cells in the process. Acidosis is thus thought to be the first step toward premature aging, accelerating oxidative cascades of cell wall destruction, creating wrinkling, age spots, dysfunctional hormonal systems, interfering with eyesight, memory, and a host of other age-related phenomena.

3. Causes Weight Gain, Diabetes and Obesity.

An acid pH has considerable influence over the majority of weight problems, including diabetes and obesity. It seems that a habitually acid pH can directly cause immediate weight gain. Here's what happens when a system is too acid. A condition known as Insulin Sensitivity or Syndrome X results, which forces too much insulin to be produced, and the body is flooded with insulin so that it won't waste any calories, it diligently converts every calorie it can into fat.

It is thought that an acid pH immediately signals the powerful genetic response to an impending famine, directly interacting with the all important and very sensitive, Insulin- Glucagon Axis. This makes the body produce more insulin than usual, and in turn, produce more fat and store it. In general, the more insulin is available to the body, the higher the probability that fat will be produced and stored, rather than used and burned as energy.

Thus, an acid pH will probably alert the genetic response to famine,

Acidosis is thus thought to be the first step toward premature aging, accelerating oxidative cascades of cell wall destruction.

An acid pH has considerable influence over the majority of weight problems, including diabetes and obesity.

directing more insulin to be produced and storing more fat than usual. Conversely, a healthy, slightly alkaline pH will be more likely to yield normal fat burning metabolic activity, making no demands on the body to overly produce insulin and make fat, allowing fat-weight to be burned and naturally lost. And, with a healthy pH, there's less likely to be any yo-yo effect, or rebounding from a diet with additional weight gain. As long as nutritional stores are maintained, a healthy, slightly alkaline pH allows fat to burn normally for energy, rather than being hoarded under the mistaken biochemical belief of an impending famine.

With increased pressure to produce insulin under the worst conditions, beta cells lose phase with one another, cellular communication is thwarted and the Immune System begins to over-respond. Stress within the cells increases, making it difficult for them to perform adequately, and further, survive. In a very real sense, they simply burn out! Acidosis is thus thought an important, yet often underestimated, precursor to Diabetes Mellitus. Interestingly, before the advent of synthetic insulin, diabetes was treated historically by buffering the system with base or alkaline causing powders.

4. Causes Cholesterol Plaque to Form.

LDL-Cholesterol is laid down at an accelerated rate within an acid chemical environment of the cardiovascular system, inappropriately lining the vascular network, and clogging up the works! The amount of cholesterol in the diet has not been found to be a major factor in cholesterol plaque formation. Rather, pH status appears to be the factor more directly involved, binding cholesterol with heavy metals and other cellular debris.

5. Disrupts Blood Pressure.

With acidosis, (pH<7.20) arteries become dilated. Yet, severe lowering of blood pH also causes persistent venous vasoconstriction (a disease in the calibre of blood vessels). When this happens, peripheral blood is shifted more centrally: the more acidic the patient, the greater the fractional redistribution of blood to the central vessels. This central redistribution of blood adds to the heart's workload when its contractibility is compromised.

In general, the more insulin is available to the body, the higher the probability that fat will be produced and stored, rather than used and burned as energy.

pH status appears to be the factor more directly involved, binding cholesterol with heavy metals and other cellular debris.

6. Disrupts Critical Lipid and Fatty Acid Metabolism.

Acidosis disrupts general lipid and fatty acid metabolism within the body. Fatty acids are intimately involved in nerve and brain function. When fatty acid metabolism is disturbed, neurological problems may arise including Multiple Sclerosis, Macular Degeneration and others, as well as problems with hormonal balance within the endocrine system.

7. Inhibits Metabolism of Stored Energy Reserves.

An acid pH inhibits efficient cellular and body metabolism. Acidosis causes chemical ionic disturbances, interfering with cellular communications and functions. Acidosis reduces Ca (calcium) binding of plasma proteins, reducing the effectiveness of this intracellular signal. Acidosis also leads to a disease of calcium cations (positive Ca) entry through positive Ca channels, resulting in reduction of cardiac contractibility, or the ability of the heart to pump efficiently and rhythmically.

Also, positive Ca and positive H (Hydrogen) regulate the activity of intracellular proteins and are driven out of cells because of the "Sodium-Potassium pump" (Na-K pump), which provides a strong incentive for sodium to be driven into cells. There are some 10 times the amount of positive Na in extra cellular fluids than in cells. The Sodium-Potassium pump regulates the amount of sodium and potassium each cell in the body stores, and uses up as much as 25% of our caloric input per day to run. Positive Ca exchanges the positive Na, being forced out of cells, but naturally, the electrochemical gradient for positive Ca favors both positive H and positive Ca entry into cells, as there is less calcium and positive H in cells than in the extra cellular fluids.

Therefore, in acid solutions, less sodium will be present, slowing down the processing and induction of nutritional items going into cells. (Calcium may become inordinately leached from bone mass, causing osteoporosis.) An acid pH drains us of energy and disallows stored energy reserves to be used. Furthermore calcium may become inordinately leached from bone mass, causing osteoporosis.

8. Inhibits Cellular Regeneration and DNA-RNA Synthesis.

For DNA-RNA synthesis and healthy cell proliferation to occur, cell pH must not be acidic. However, cancerous cells grow well in acidic

> When fatty acid metabolism is disturbed, neurological problems may arise including Multiple Sclerosis, Macular Degeneration and others.

> Acidosis causes chemical ionic disturbances, interfering with cellular communications and functions.

mediums, therefore an acid pH actually accelerates and increases the possibility of cellular mutations (Cancer).

CANCEROUS CELLS DO NOT CONTAIN HYDROGEN ATOMS. WHEN HEALTHY CELLS HAVE PLENTY OF HYDROGEN THEY CANNOT BECOME CANCEROUS. IF WE CAN GET HYDROGEN INTO ANY UNHEALTHY CELLS, THEY CAN HEAL.

9. Inhibits Oxygen Getting to the Tissue.

Acidosis or an acid pH decreases the amount of oxygen that can be delivered to cells, making normally healthy cells unhealthy so eventually they die.

10. Inhibits Life Giving Electrolyte Activity.

Life-essential functions, like electrolyte Potassium (K plus) and Sodium (Na plus) channels, are inactivated by acidosis. This has far reaching effects cardiovascularly, since without sufficient electrolyte management, heart attacks are likely to occur. Without appropriate electrolyte management, our heart literally stops beating. Inhibition of electrolyte activity also affects the way we feel and behave, and is intimately involved in the energy levels we experience because of the nature of the Na-K Pump and cellular metabolism.

Cancerous cells grow well in acidic mediums, therefore an acid pH actually accelerates and increases the possibility of cellular mutations (Cancer).

More Symptoms of Acidosis

Due to fast paced daily lifestyles, eating on the run, people have to face a constantly growing endangerment: the over-acidification (**acidosis**) of the body cells, which will interrupt cellular activities and functions. It is a major root of sickness and disease. Having our cells constantly exposed to an **acidic environment** leads to **acidosis**!

Studies have shown that an acidic, **anaerobic** (which is also the lack of oxygen) body environment encourages the breeding of fungus, mold, bacteria, and viruses. As a result, our inner biological terrain shifts from a healthy oxygenated, **alkaline environment** to an unhealthy acidic one (acidic pH scale).

It is a lot of "hard work" for our body to neutralize and **detoxify** these acids before they can act as poisons in and around the cells, ultimately changing the environment of each cell.

When our **body pH** becomes more and more acidic it starts to set up defense mechanisms to keep the damaging acid from entering our vital organs. **Unhealthy conditions which can be caused directly by Over-Acidification/Acidosis are:**

Symptom: OVERWEIGHT

It is known that acid gets stored in fat cells. As a defense mechanism, your body may actually produce fat cells to protect you from your overly acidic condition. To protect itself from potentially serious damage, the body creates these fat cells to store the acids and carry them away from vital organs. Those fat cells and cellulite deposits may actually keep acid wastes at a safe distance from your vital organs. Many people have found that a return to a healthy alkaline inner biological terrain helps them losing excess fat.

Symptom: JOINT PAIN AND ARTHRITIS

All substances left by the metabolizing process are acidic and toxic; therefore, these have to be neutralized by alkalizing elements, e.g. calcium ions, sodium ions, and lithium ions, among which calcium is the most important. Calcium ions are positively charged ions which are constantly looking for acid, to form calcium carbonate in our body. Calcium carbonate is harmless and will be moved out of the body, providing our body fluid pH is alkaline. Otherwise, it is being deposited around body joints. If the calcium ion level is low in the blood and body, excess acid will remain in our body and will lead to numerous

As a defense mechanism, your body may actually produce fat cells to protect you from your overly acidic condition.

All substances left by the metabolizing process are acidic and toxic.

health problems, like joint pain or rrthritis.

Symptom: OSTEOPOROSIS

Many people think they can eliminate osteoporosis by increasing their consumption of milk and dairy products. But, in fact, the instances of osteoporosis are rare in countries where the consumption of dairy products is very low. So osteoporosis is an acidosis problem. As the body becomes more acidic, our body tries to remain healthy to protect us against heart attacks, illness, strokes, or even cancer. In doing so, it takes calcium from the teeth, bones, and tissues, making them weak and brittle.

Symptom: UNDERWEIGHT

Yeast and fungus produced in an acidic environment can feed on our nutrients and thus reduce the absorption of everything we eat by as much as 50%. Without protein the body can't produce enzymes, hormones or other chemical components necessary for cell energy and organ activity. This causes people to become very thin, which is not healthier than being overweight. As alkalizing and oxygenating takes place, the body naturally begins to seek its own ideal weight.

Symptom: LOW ENERGY AND CHRONIC FATIGUE

When having our cells constantly exposed to an overly acidic environment our biological terrain's oxygen level drops, leaving us tired and fatigued. This will allow parasites, fungus, bacteria, mold, and viral infections to flourish and gain a hold throughout the body.

Symptom: HEART ATTACK

If our internal biological terrain is exposed to excessive acidity, bacteria and/or fungi and/or viruses can attach themselves to the inner walls of arteries. This can attract white blood cells causing proteins and cells to clot. In this way a plaque forms in the artery, thus narrowing the artery and restricting the flow of blood, nutrients, and oxygen to the tissues supplied by that artery. Should that happen to the coronary artery, a heart attack can occur.

Symptom: ALLERGIES

The toxins produced within an acidic, oxygen deprived environment as well as the absorption of undigested proteins is major cause of allergy conditions. When the digestive system is weakened, a wide range of allergic reactions can occur, e.g. food allergies, and the overall susceptibility to allergens is increased.

As the body becomes more acidic, our body tries to remain healthy to protect us against heart attacks, illness, strokes or even cancer. In doing so, it takes calcium from the teeth, bones, and tissues, making them weak and brittle.

When the digestive system is weakened, a wide range of allergic reactions can occur, e.g. food allergies, and the overall susceptibility to allergens is increased.

Symptom: ACNE

There are many different forms of acne, and not few are linked to an unhealthy diet. Especially foods that are highly acidic tend to cause acne.

Symptom: FREQUENT COLDS, BRONCHITIS, INFECTIONS, HEADACHES

Only when our pH level is fairly balanced, the binding of oxygen to the hemoglobin protein of our red blood cells in the lungs operates. If the pH is too acidic, microbes in our respiratory systems can grow much more easily, and in that way cause bronchitis, pneumonia, and sinusitis, and invade our cell system. This can result in cough, bronchial spasms (asthma), colds, infections, and headaches.

Foods that are highly acidic tend to cause acne.

If the pH is too acidic, microbes in our respiratory systems can grow much more easily, and in that way cause bronchitis, pneumonia, and sinusitis, and invade our cell system.

A Nasty Consequence of an Overly Acidic Body

The acid waste also sets the stage for the potentially devastating effects of a host of microscopic organisms in your body, starting with *Candida*. Candida is the Latin name for what is commonly known as a yeast in the human body but is really a kind of fungus. Yeast and fungus (and the closely related mold) are single-celled forms of plant life that inhabit land, air, and water. They are absolutely everywhere. For example, Candida is normally found in the gastrointestinal tract. We'd actually die without it.

However, it can easily become drastically overgrown, causing a wide variety of symptoms, from annoying to chronic to fatal. This is the bug all too many women are familiar with through "yeast infection," and parents may have experience with if their infants ever had thrush (which is just Candida growing in the throat).

While mainstream medicine recognizes these and a handful of other medical problems stemming from yeast and fungus, the truth is that on the typical American diet the vast majority of people develop out-of-control growths within their bodies — and the effects are disastrous.

Actually, Candida is just one of the villains. We are living in a plague of "microforms," including yeasts, fungus, and molds as well as bacteria and viruses. Worse still, we are victimized not only by the microforms themselves, but also by their poisonous excretions, or "mycotoxins" and "exotoxins" (from "myco," meaning fungus, "exo," meaning bacterial, and "toxin," meaning, of course, poison). The microforms produce these acidic wastes when they digest (ferment, really) glucose, proteins, and fats — the same substances our bodies are looking to use for energy.

Candida and other microforms take advantage of the body's weaker areas, poisoning and overworking them. In an acidic environment, they basically get free rein to break down tissues and bodily processes. They live on our body's glucose, which they use for energy, and use our fats and proteins (even our genetic matter, nucleic acids!) for development and growth. These organisms are literally eating us alive! They then send their waste products (acids) out into the bloodstream, as well as inside the cells, further polluting the system.

Candida can easily become drastically overgrown, causing a wide variety of symptoms, from annoying to chronic to fatal.

Candida and other microforms basically get free rein to break down tissues and bodily processes.

Just to give you a little perspective on just how daunting the potential damage is: Over the hundreds of millions of years that yeast, fungus, and mold have been on earth, they have developed into over five hundred thousand different identifiable forms. And they've undergone little genetic change. Apparently, they haven't needed to because they are great opportunists and survivalists, perfectly suited to what they do. They can go from explosive growth to thousands of years of dormancy. (Living spores have been found in ancient Egyptian tombs only recently excavated.) Furthermore, there are more than a thousand toxins produced by yeast, fungus, and mold.

What Symptoms May Be Caused By Candida?

In the **First Stage of Candida**, the mucous membrane areas of the body may be infected. These include the mouth, vagina, nose, and respiratory System. Besides vaginal infections, severe P.M.S., urinary tract infections, body rashes, acne, and oral thrush, ALLERGIES to foods, dust, molds, fungus, yeast, inhalants, and chemicals are the most common symptoms. Each day more people seem to be allergic to everything in their environment. Repeated bouts of bronchitis, sinusitis, tonsillitis, and strep or staph infections may be typical. Mononucleosis and pneumonia may also be noted. It is easy to perceive that each of these successive illnesses requires more and more antibiotics, which may open the door for further Candida overgrowth.

Talk about a vicious circle!

The **Second Stage of Candida** may involve more generalized reactions such as PAIN, HEADACHES (including MIGRAINE), EXTREME FATIGUE, PSORIASIS, INFECTIONS OF THE NAILS, MUSCLE ACHES, JOINT PAINS, AND ARTHRITIS. Naturally, drug after drug is usually taken in hopes of alleviating these miserable conditions. In most cases, the SYMPTOMS alone are being treated—while the CAUSE (candida overgrowth) may be literally being PROMOTED at the same time!

The **Third Stage of Candida** may involve MENTAL and BEHAVIORAL responses: inability to concentrate, not being able to read or follow a television program or carry on a hobby, serious forgetfulness, memory loss, mental confusion, not being able to think of the words to say something, switching around of words and letters when trying to speak and/or write something, loss of previous skills (such as how-to-type or how-to-play-the-piano, etc.) These frightening problems may often lead to "HOPELESS CRYING" SPELLS, SEVERE DEPRESSION, SLEEP

DISORDERS (may include insomnia, confusion dreams, nightmares, apnea, and not feeling rested or restored after sleep), IRRATIONAL THOUGHTS, UNUSUAL FEARS, PHOBIAS, PANIC/ANXIETY ATTACKS, MUSCLE TWITCHING, IRRITABILITY, VIOLENCE, AGGRESSIVE BEHAVIOR, and even EPILEPTIC SEIZURES and THOUGHTS OF DEATH OR SUICIDE.

Sometimes people with these symptoms are labeled "mentally ill", thought to be suffering from manic-depressive psychosis or schizophrenia. These desperately sick patients are sometimes turned over to the care of a psychiatrist or hospitalized in a mental institution. They may be given antidepressants, tranquilizers, lithium, etc. to lighten the mental symptoms. But the cause may be overlooked and the patient is not cured on a long-term basis.

A person in the **Fourth Stage of Candida** may experience a virtual SHUTDOWN OF VARIOUS ORGAN SYSTEMS of the body. For example, the adrenal glands may stop functioning when the endocrine system fails, or the digestive system may stop, producing vomiting or severe constipation. The extreme fatigue may escalate into TOTAL MUSCLE WEAKNESS, such as the neck muscles no longer being able to hold up the head. The body rashes may escalate into HIVES or BOILS.

The circulatory system may be swamped with so much yeast that the capillaries are clogged, causing HIGH BLOOD PRESSURE, NUMBNESS OF EXTREMITIES, and EASY BRUISING. The person may run a low-grade fever, but the hands and feet will often be very cold. The HEART may develop TACHYCARDIA (palpitations, irregular beats, mitral valve problems or heart murmur).

In the respiratory system, the alveoli (air sacs) of the lungs may be packed with yeast so that the person cannot get adequate breath for speaking, singing, or exercise; there may be a FEELING OF SUFFOCATION, which may lead to HYPERVENTILATION and PANIC. The complete failure of the immune system leaves the body defenseless against all enemy bacteria, viruses, and disease conditions — including cancer.

The **Fifth Stage of Candida** seems inevitable at this point: rampant systemic Candidiasis is 100% fatal unless it is diagnosed early enough to kill the yeast overgrowth and regenerate the immune system.

Sometimes people with these symptoms are labeled "mentally ill", thought to be suffering from manic-depressive psychosis or schizophrenia.

The complete failure of the immune system leaves the body defenseless against all enemy bacteria, viruses, and disease conditions— including cancer.

The Single Underlying Cause of All Disease.

The old biology, based on the work of Louis Pasteur in the late 1800s, stems from the idea that disease comes from germs which invade the body from the outside. In contrast Dr. Robert O. Young has found that when the body is in healthy alkaline balance, germs are unable to get a foothold.

Think of your body as a fish tank. Think of the importance of maintaining the integrity of the internal fluids of the body that we swim in daily. Imagine the fish in this tank are your cells and organ systems bathed in fluids, which transport food and remove wastes.

Now imagine we back up a car and put the tailpipe up against the air intake filter that supplies the oxygen for the water in the tank. The water becomes filled with carbon monoxide, lowering the alkaline pH, creating and acidic pH environment, and threatening the health of the fish, your cells and organs.

What if we throw in too much food or the wrong kind of food (acid-producing food like dairy, sugar, and animal protein) and the fish are unable to consume or digest it all, and it starts to decompose and putrefy? Toxic acid waste and chemicals build up as the food breaks down, creating more acidic byproducts, altering the optimum alkaline pH.

Basically, this is a small example of what we may be doing to our internal fluids every day. We are fouling them with pollution (smoking), drugs, excessive intake of food, over-consumption of acid-forming foods (dairy food, sugar, animal protein), and any number of transgressions which compromise the delicate balance of our internal alkaline fluids.

Some of us have fish tanks (bodies) that are barely able to support life, yet we somehow manage to struggle from day to day, building more severe imbalances until there is the inevitable crash and debilitating chronic, disturbing and disorganizing symptoms to deal with.

The pH level (the acid-alkaline measurement) of our internal fluids affects every cell in our bodies. Extended acid imbalances of any kind are not well tolerated by the body. Indeed, the entire metabolic process depends on a balanced internal alkaline environment. A chronically over-acidic pH corrodes body tissue, slowly eating into the

When the body is in healthy alkaline balance, germs are unable to get a foothold.

The pH level (the acid-alkaline measurement) of our internal fluids affects every cell in our bodies.

91

Over-acidification interferes with life itself leading to all sickness and disease.

60,000 miles of veins and arteries like acid eating into marble. If left unchecked, it will interrupt all cellular activities and functions, from the beating of your heart to the neural firing of your brain.

In summary, over-acidification interferes with life itself leading to all sickness and disease.

Monitoring Your Body pH

We suggest that one monitor their Body pH Level on at least a weekly basis. Monitor daily if you so desire. It is a good practice to be aware of the Alkaline/Acid condition of your body. The pH is measured by a urine or saliva test… which is very simple to do and requires less than a minute of your time.

The best way to monitor the Body pH Level… is by using a Digital pH Meter. This will give you an exact reading from 0 to 14 pH Levels... so that you can monitor when your body pH is exactly between 7.1 and 7.3. Digital pH Meters are available in most hydroponics stores. The other option available… is to use Hydrion pH Testing Strips which are available through most drug stores and some health food stores. These are color coded into a general pH range… and you should look for test strips that will register **half-point increments**.

How to Test Your pH Level

Test your pH level... If you are sick or have cancer simply wet a piece of Litmus Paper with your saliva 2 hours after a meal. This will give a reflection of your state of health.

Salivary pH Test: While generally more acidic than blood, salivary pH mirrors the blood (if not around meals) and is also a fairly good indicator of health. It tells us what the body retains. Salivary pH is a fair indicator of the health of the extra cellular fluids and their alkaline mineral reserves.

Optimal pH for saliva is 6.4 to 6.8. Spit upon arising before anything is put into the mouth. A reading lower than 6.4 is indicative of insufficient alkaline reserves. Two hours after eating, on testing — the saliva pH should rise to 7.8 or higher. Unless this occurs, the body has alkaline mineral deficiencies (mainly Calcium and Magnesium) and will not assimilate food very well. To deviate from ideal salivary pH for an extended time invites illness.

Acidosis, an extended time in the acid pH state, can result in rheumatoid arthritis, diabetes, lupus, tuberculosis, osteoporosis, high blood pressure, most cancers, and many more heath problems. If salivary pH stays too low, the diet should focus on fruit, vegetables, and still mineral water as well as

> It is a good practice to monitor your pH level at least once weekly.

> Optimal pH for saliva is 6.4 to 6.8. A reading lower than 6.4 is indicative of insufficient alkaline reserves.

removing strong acidifiers such as sodas, whole wheat, and red meat.

Urinary pH Test: The pH of the urine indicates how the body is working to maintain the proper pH of the blood. The urine reveals the alkaline building (anabolic) and acid tearing down (catabolic) cycles. The pH of urine indicates the efforts of the body via the kidneys, adrenals, lungs, and gonads to regulate pH through the buffer salts and hormones. Urine can provide a fairly accurate picture of body chemistry because the kidneys filter out the buffer salts of pH regulation and provide values based on what the body is eliminating. Urine pH can vary from around 4.5 to 9.0 for its extremes, but the ideal range is 5.8 to 6.8.

Urine pH can vary from around 4.5 to 9.0 for its extremes, but the ideal range is 5.8 to 6.8.

pH is Vital for Whole Body Health

Finding the Right Balance

At the first mention of acidity and alkalinity, eyes glaze over. After all, these terms sound somewhat scientific, and vague memories of junior high science class and litmus paper changing color may come to mind. However, the balance between acidity and alkalinity, and its importance, can be explained quite simply and should be explained. This balance is essential to good health.

The Basics

Every solution is either acidic or alkaline. (Alkaline is often called "base.") These solutions can be anything from body fluids, such as stomach acid and blood, to beverages, such as wine or coffee, to sea water. Acidity and alkalinity are measured in pH (potential of hydrogen). The pH scale goes from 0 to 14, with 0 the most acidic, and 14 the most alkaline. The pH of stomach acid is 1, wine is 3.5, water is 7 (neutral), venous blood is 7.35, arterial blood is 7.4, sea water is 8.5, and baking soda is 12. Ideally, our pH should stay on the alkaline side: between 7.35 and 7.45.

Keeping our acidity and alkalinity balanced means regulating the hydrogen ion concentration in our body fluids. An acid is a molecule or ion (an ion is an atom that carries a positive or negative electric charge) that can contribute a hydrogen ion to a solution. An alkalizing substance is one that contains a molecule or ion that combines with hydrogen ions to remove them from a solution it neutralizes acids and acts as a buffer.

The Misconceptions

Foods are classified as acid-forming or alkalizing depending on the effect they have on the body. An acid-forming food contributes hydrogen ions to the body, making it more acidic. An alkalizing food removes hydrogen ions from the body, making it more alkaline. It is important to note that this classification is based on the effect foods have on the body after digestion, not on their own intrinsic acidity or alkalinity (or how they taste to us).

A common misconception is that if a food tastes acidic, it has an acid-forming effect on the body. This is not necessarily true. Very often, an acidic-tasting food is alkalizing. Citric fruits are a good example. People say that lemons, for example, are "too acidic"; however, they are actually alkalizing because the minerals they leave behind after digestion help remove hydrogen ions, decreasing the acidity of the body. (Many people use the term "residue" or "ash" to explain the effect of a food on the body. A food with an acid ash after digestion contributes hydrogen ions, making the body more acidic; a food with an alkaline ash after digestion removes hydrogen ions, making the body more alkaline.)

Another misconception is that acid-forming foods are "bad." This is not correct; acidity and alkalinity are opposites and one is not intrinsically better than the other. This misconception has developed because the North American diet is excessively acidic, which does result in health problems.

Common acid-forming foods include processed junk foods and those that are high in animal protein. Some common alkalizing foods are spinach, soybeans, raisins, carrots, and most citrus fruits.

The Problem

Looking at this short list of acid-forming and alkalizing foods, you can see where the problem lies. North Americans eat considerably more acid-forming foods than alkalizing foods. Unfortunately, too much acid can cause health problems. According to well-known naturopath Paavo Airola in his book "How to Get Well", Acidosis, or over-acidity in the body tissues, is one of the basic causes of diseases, especially the arthritic and rheumatic diseases."

Others concur with Airola. Speaking of the acidity of a high-fat, high-sugar diet, Michael Colgan, in The New Nutrition, says, "Acidosis destroys bones, because the body has to steal alkalizing minerals from them, to keep the blood pH from dropping into the acid range. " Dr. Mary Ruth Swope, in Green Leaves of Barley, comments, "We have become too full of acid and, as a result, are experiencing a wide range of diseases that flourish in the acid medium." Dr. Yoshihide Hagiwara, in Green Barley Essence, mentions that, "Should this balance (acid and alkaline) be upset, the cell metabolism suffers, leading to conditions such as fatigue."

Common symptoms of an unbalanced pH include heartburn (a burning sensation in the stomach and acid-tasting burps), bloating, belching, and feeling full after eating small amounts of food. Other symptoms could include insomnia, water retention, migraines, constipation with diarrhea, fatigue, a burning sensation on the tongue and in the mouth, and halitosis.

The Solution

Eat a diet that helps your body maintain the correct acidity-alkalinity balance. According to Airola, the ideal diet should have a natural ratio of four parts alkaline to one part acid. Others contend that while this a good ratio for active people (exercise creates a lot of acid), less active people can handle a diet with a ratio of two parts alkaline to one part acid.

The ideal diet should have a natural ratio of four parts alkaline to one part acid.

Alkalizing Testimonials

I am 81 years old, my blood pressure went from 140 to 120/70!

Harvette H, West Chester, OH

In 4 months I dropped from 3 sizes. My knees do not hurt anymore, elbows don't hurt, and complexion has changed. My dogs prefer alkaline water; one dog's ear infection is gone. (A month later.) The tumor on my mother's neck started to drain about 5 weeks ago.

Leslie L., West St Paul, MN

In 4 months I lost 10 lbs. All my friends commented on how good I look.

Romy S., Miami, FL

In 7 days my blood pressure went down!

Ken W., Miami, FL

It helped my eyes right away, dissolved the cataracts. Better complexion, lines are gone!

Pat A., Kalamazoo, MI

(AFTER 16 months) Just got results of blood test from my doctor, he said, 'No trace of Diabetes in your blood!'

Sandra B., Oak Park, IL

For the first time in my life my cholesterol went down from over 200 to 160!

Winnie T., Miami, FL

Let thy food be thy medicine, and thy medicine be thy food.

Hippocrates, Father of Medicine, 400 B.C.

SECTION TWO:

The Deadliest Acid?

SUGAR: A History

Shipwrecked sailors who ate and drank nothing but sugar and rum for nine days surely went through some of this trauma; the tales they had to tell created a big public relations problem for the sugar pushers. This incident occurred when a vessel carrying a cargo of sugar was shipwrecked in 1793. The five surviving sailors were finally rescued after being marooned for nine days. They were in a wasted condition due to starvation, having consumed nothing but sugar and rum. The eminent French physiologist F. Magendie was inspired by that incident to conduct a series of experiments with animals, the results of which he published in 1816. In the experiments, he fed dogs a diet of sugar or olive oil and water. All the dogs wasted and died.

The shipwrecked sailors and the French physiologist's experimental dogs proved the same point. As a steady diet, sugar is worse than nothing. Plain water can keep you alive for quite some time. Sugar and water can kill you. Humans (and animals) are "unable to subsist on a diet of sugar." The dead dogs in Professor Magendie's laboratory alerted the sugar industry to the hazards of free scientific inquiry. From that day to this, the sugar industry has invested millions of dollars in behind-the-scenes, subsidized science. The best scientific names that money could buy have been hired, in the hope that they could one day come up with something at least pseudoscientific in the way of glad tidings about sugar.

It has been proved, however, that sugar is a major factor in dental decay; sugar in a person's diet does cause overweight; removal of sugar from diets has cured symptoms of crippling, worldwide diseases such as diabetes, cancer, and heart illnesses. Sir Frederick Banting, the co-discoverer of insulin, noticed in 1929 in Panama that, among sugar plantation owners who ate large amounts of their refined stuff, diabetes was common. Among native cane-cutters, who only got to chew the raw cane, he saw no diabetes. However, the story of the public relations attempts on the part of the sugar manufacturers began in Britain in 1808 when the Committee of West India reported to the House of Commons that a prize of twenty-five guineas had been offered to anyone who could come up with the most "satisfactory" experiments to prove that unrefined sugar was good for feeding and fattening oxen, cows, hogs and sheep.

Food for animals is often

As a steady diet, sugar is worse than nothing. Plain water can keep you alive for quite some time. Sugar and water can kill you.

Sir Frederick Banting, the co-discoverer of insulin, noticed in 1929 in Panama that, among sugar plantation owners who ate large amounts of their refined stuff, diabetes was common.

seasonal, always expensive. Sugar, by then, was dirt cheap. People weren't eating it fast enough. Naturally, the attempt to feed livestock with sugar and molasses in England in 1808 was a disaster. When the Committee on West India made its fourth report to the House of Commons, one Member of Parliament, John Curwin, reported that he had tried to feed sugar and molasses to calves without success. He suggested that perhaps someone should try again by sneaking sugar and molasses into skimmed milk. Had anything come of that, you can be sure the West Indian sugar merchants would have spread the news around the world. After this singular lack of success in pushing sugar in cow pastures, the West Indian sugar merchants gave up.

With undaunted zeal for increasing the market demand for the most important agricultural product of the West Indies, the Committee of West India was reduced to a tactic that has served the sugar pushers for almost 200 years: irrelevant and transparently silly testimonials from faraway, inaccessible people with some kind of "scientific" credentials. While preparing his epochal volume, A History of Nutrition, published in 1957, Professor E. V. McCollum (Johns Hopkins university), sometimes called America's foremost nutritionist and certainly a pioneer in the field, reviewed approximately 200,000 published scientific papers,

recording experiments with food, their properties, their utilization, and their effects on animals and men. The material covered the period from the mid-18th century to 1940. From this great repository of scientific inquiry, McCollum selected those experiments which he regarded as significant "to relate the story of progress in discovering human error in this segment of science (of nutrition)".

Professor McCollum failed to record a single controlled scientific experiment with sugar between 1816 and 1940. Unhappily, we must remind ourselves that scientists today, and always, accomplish little without a sponsor. The protocols of modern science have compounded the costs of scientific inquiry. We have no right to be surprised when we read the introduction to McCollum's A History of Nutrition and find that "The author and publishers are indebted to The Nutrition Foundation, Inc., for a grant provided to meet a portion of the cost of publication of this book". What, you might ask, is The Nutrition Foundation, Inc.? The author and the publishers don't tell you. It happens to be a front organization for the leading sugar-pushing conglomerates in the food business, including the American Sugar Refining Company, Coca-Cola, Pepsi-Cola, Curtis Candy Co., General Foods, General Mills, Nestlé Co., Pet Milk Co. and Sunshine Biscuits — about 45 such companies in all. Perhaps the most significant thing about McCollum's 1957 history was what he left out: a monumental earlier work described by an eminent Harvard professor as "one of those epochal pieces of research which makes every other investigator desirous of kicking himself because he never thought of doing the same thing".

In the 1930s, a research dentist from Cleveland, Ohio, Dr. Weston A. Price, traveled all over the world-from the lands of the Eskimos to the South Sea Islands, from Africa to New Zealand. His Nutrition and Physical Degeneration: A Comparison of Primitive and Modern Diets and Their Effects which is illustrated with hundreds of photographs, was first published in 1939. Dr. Price took the whole world as his laboratory. His devastating conclusion, recorded in horrifying detail in area after area, was simple. People who live under so-called backward primitive conditions had excellent teeth and wonderful general health. They ate natural, unrefined food from their own locale. As soon as refined, sugared foods were imported as a result of contact with "civilization," physical degeneration began in a way that was definitely observable within a single generation. Any credibility the sugar pushers have is based on our ignorance of works like that of Dr. Price.

Sugar manufacturers keep trying, hoping, and contributing generous research grants to colleges and universities; but the research laboratories never come up with anything solid the manufacturers can use. Invariably, the research results are bad news. "Let us go to the ignorant savage, consider his way of eating and be wise," Harvard professor Ernest Hooten said in Apes, Men, and Morons. "Let us cease pretending that toothbrushes and toothpaste are any more important than shoe brushes and shoe polish. It is store food that has given us store teeth."

When the researchers bite the hands that feed them, and the news gets out, it's embarrassing all around. In 1958, Time magazine reported that a Harvard biochemist and his assistants had worked with myriads of mice for more than ten years, bankrolled by the Sugar Research Foundation, Inc. to the tune of $57,000, to find out how sugar causes dental cavities and how to prevent this. It took them ten years to discover that there was no way to prevent sugar causing dental decay. When the researchers reported their findings in the Dental Association Journal, their source of money dried up. The Sugar Research Foundation withdrew its support. The more that the scientists disappointed them, the more the sugar pushers had to rely on the ad men.

People who live under so-called backward primitive conditions had excellent teeth and wonderful general health. They ate natural, unrefined food from their own locale.

It took them ten years to discover that there was no way to prevent sugar causing dental decay.

105

Sugar: Addiction and Dangers

Human researchers are fascinated by the behavior of lab rats in response to food rewards, but few humans are willing to closely examine their own behavior in relationship to sugar. Most people living in western societies (the U.S., Canada, UK, Australia, etc.) are truly addicted to sugar, and they use it as a form of self-medication to temporarily boost their mood and energy. The frequency and context in which these people press a button on a soda machine is eerily similar to the way lab rats press a lever to produce a food reward.

> Most people living in western societies (the U.S., Canada, UK, Australia, etc.) are truly addicted to sugar, and they use it as a form of self-medication to temporarily boost their mood and energy.

This CounterThink cartoon attempts to ask, "What would an outside observer think of modern human behavior in relation to sugar?" The answer is not difficult to predict: They would think humans were strange animals to be so utterly controlled by a crystalline white substance. Refined white sugar is like dietary crack, and it rots out your teeth just like meth, only slower.

Of course, most people reading this cartoon will insist, "I'm not addicted to sugar. I can quit eating sugar anytime I want." Really? Prove it! See if you can go sugar-free for just ten days. That's a real eye-opener for most people because even if they have the determination to attempt such an experiment, most soon find themselves crawling back to the pantry, desperately seeking a soda beverage loaded with high-fructose corn syrup (liquid sugar) to end their withdrawal symptoms.

The truth is, most American consumers are so addicted to sugar that they will deny their addictions in the same way that a crack or heroin addict might.

The truth is, most American consumers are so addicted to sugar that they will deny their addictions in the same way that a crack or heroin addict might. And yet, when it comes down to it, sugar controls their behavior. If they don't have their sugar in the morning (in their coffee, pancakes, and cereals), sugar at lunch (in the salad dressing, pasta sauce, soda and restaurant food) and sugar at dinner (there's sugar in pizza, ketchup, and BBQ sauce, plus virtually all restaurant foods), then they suffer serious withdrawal symptoms and go crazy with moodiness and irritability. They start blaming everyone around them for silly things, and they may even become sweaty and light-headed.

Curious, isn't it? That's what happens when you take a substance out of nature and refine it to maximize its chemical surface area and biological activity. Cocaine is a drug that's refined from coca leaves. Opium is a drug that's refined from poppies. And sugar is a drug that's refined from sugarcane. And while we have a "war on drugs" against cocaine and heroin, our taxpayer dollars actually subsidize the sugar industry, making refined white sugar cheap and widely available to the entire population so that everyone can be equally hooked.

Refined white sugar is a pleasure drug. If you don't believe me, just put a spoonful on your tongue and observe the instantaneous effects. You'll experience a warming, comfortable feeling that makes you feel safe and happy. They're not called "comfort foods" by accident.

Sugar is, essentially, a legalized recreational drug that's socially acceptable to consume. And yet, just like other drugs, it destroys a person's health.

Sugar is, essentially, a legalized recreational drug that's socially acceptable to consume. And yet, just like other drugs, it destroys a person's health over time, rotting out their teeth, disrupting normal brain function, promoting heart disease, and directly causing diabetes and obesity. The argument that "street drugs are outlawed because they're dangerous to a person's health" falls flat on its face when you consider what sugar does to the human body. It's a lot more dangerous than marijuana, for example, and yet marijuana is illegal to possess or consume.

Isn't it curious how, in modern society, we fight a war against certain drugs (like cocaine), yet subsidize others? (Like sugar.) The difference, of course, is that the sugar industry has a powerful political lobby and is universally abused by virtually the entire population. Drugs that are abused by only a few (such as heroin) get outlawed, while drugs that are abused by everyone (such as caffeine and sugar) receive legal immunity. It's mob rule. And the mob is addicted to sugar.

There's the old saying that sugar is poison. Americans each consume more than 150 pounds of sugar and related sweeteners each year. It's pretty easy for it to add up when you consider that there are 17 teaspoons of sugar in a single can of Coke. Author Nancy Appleton delineates how this sugar over-consumption wreaks havoc with our immune and endocrine systems, leading to chronic conditions including arthritis, osteoporosis, diabetes, asthma, and hypoglycemia, along with the usual suspects such as cavities and periodontal disease. Appleton admits that she herself used to be a sugar addict, preferring to take her sweets in the form of chocolate, and consequently suffered from numerous allergies, plus bronchitis, pneumonia, and even a chest tumor that turned out to be a huge calcium deposit that resulted from her body's inability to process the pounds of sugar she consumed.

While Appleton has a Ph.D. and has been studying nutrition for years, she doesn't go into unnecessary scientific details when she explains what those little sugar cubes do to your body. This is a thoroughly readable, eye-opening guide to changing your diet — and your health — for the better.

76 Ways Sugar Can Ruin Your Health

Contributed by Nancy Appleton, Ph.D

In addition to throwing off the body's homeostasis, excess sugar may result in a number of other significant consequences. The following is a listing of some of sugar's metabolic consequences from a variety of medical journals and other scientific publications.

1. Sugar can suppress your immune system and impair your defenses against infectious disease.

2. Sugar upsets the mineral relationships in your body: causes chromium and copper deficiencies and interferes with absorption of calcium and magnesium.

3. Sugar can cause can cause a rapid rise of adrenaline, hyperactivity,

> Americans each consume more than 150 pounds of sugar and related sweeteners each year.

> Sugar can suppress your immune system and impair your defenses against infectious disease.

109

anxiety, difficulty concentrating, and crankiness in children.

Sugar feeds cancer
cells and has been
connected with the
development of
cancer of the
breast, ovaries,
prostate, rectum,
pancreas, biliary
tract, lung,
gallbladder and
stomach.

4. Sugar can produce a significant rise in total cholesterol, triglycerides and bad cholesterol and a decrease in good cholesterol.

5. Sugar causes a loss of tissue elasticity and function.

6. Sugar feeds cancer cells and has been connected with the development of cancer of the breast, ovaries, prostate, rectum, pancreas, biliary tract, lung, gallbladder, and stomach.

7. Sugar can increase fasting levels of glucose and can cause reactive hypoglycemia.

8. Sugar can weaken eyesight.

9. Sugar can cause many problems with the gastrointestinal tract including: an acidic digestive tract, indigestion, malabsorption in patients with functional bowel disease, increased risk of Crohn's disease, and ulcerative colitis.

10. Sugar can cause premature aging.

11. Sugar can lead to alcoholism.

12. Sugar can cause your saliva to become acidic, tooth decay, and periodontal disease.

13. Sugar contributes to obesity.

Sugar can cause
autoimmune
diseases such as:
arthritis, asthma,
multiple sclerosis.

14. Sugar can cause autoimmune diseases such as: arthritis, asthma, multiple sclerosis.

15. Sugar greatly assists the uncontrolled growth of Candida Albicans (yeast infections)

16. Sugar can cause gallstones.

17. Sugar can cause appendicitis.

18. Sugar can cause hemorrhoids.

19. Sugar can cause varicose veins.

20. Sugar can elevate glucose and insulin responses in oral contraceptive users.

21. Sugar can contribute to osteoporosis.

22. Sugar can cause a decrease in your insulin sensitivity thereby causing an abnormally high insulin levels and eventually diabetes.

23. Sugar can lower your Vitamin E levels.

24. Sugar can increase your systolic blood pressure.

25. Sugar can cause drowsiness and decreased activity in children.

26. High sugar intake increases advanced glycation end products (AGEs) (Sugar molecules attaching to and thereby damaging proteins in the body).

27. Sugar can interfere with your absorption of protein.

28. Sugar causes food allergies.

29. Sugar can cause toxemia during pregnancy.

30. Sugar can contribute to eczema in children.

31. Sugar can cause atherosclerosis and cardiovascular disease.

32. Sugar can impair the structure of your DNA.

33. Sugar can change the structure of protein and cause a permanent alteration of the way the proteins act in your body.

34. Sugar can make your skin age by changing the structure of collagen.

35. Sugar can cause cataracts and nearsightedness.

36. Sugar can cause emphysema.

37. High sugar intake can impair the physiological homeostasis of many systems in your body.

38. Sugar lowers the ability of enzymes to function.

39. Sugar intake is higher in people with Parkinson's disease.

40. Sugar can increase the size of your liver by making your liver cells divide and it can increase the amount of liver fat.

Sugar can contribute to osteoporosis.

Sugar can interfere with your absorption of protein.

Sugar can impair the structure of your DNA.

Sugar can damage
your pancreas.

Sugar can cause an
increase in delta,
alpha, and theta
brain waves which
can alter your
mind's ability to
think clearly.

Sugar can cause
depression.

High sucrose diets
of subjects with
peripheral vascular
disease significantly
increases platelet
adhesion.

41. Sugar can increase kidney size and produce pathological changes in the kidney such as the formation of kidney stones.

42. Sugar can damage your pancreas.

43. Sugar can increase your body's fluid retention.

44. Sugar is enemy #1 of your bowel movement.

45. Sugar can compromise the lining of your capillaries.

46. Sugar can make your tendons more brittle.

47. Sugar can cause headaches, including migraines.

48. Sugar can reduce the learning capacity, adversely affect school children's grades and cause learning disorders.

49. Sugar can cause an increase in delta, alpha, and theta brain waves which can alter your mind's ability to think clearly.

50. Sugar can cause depression.

51. Sugar can increase your risk of gout.

52. Sugar can increase your risk of Alzheimer's disease.

53. Sugar can cause hormonal imbalances such as: increasing estrogen in men, exacerbating PMS, and decreasing growth hormone.

54. Sugar can lead to dizziness.

55. Diets high in sugar will increase free radicals and oxidative stress.

56. High sucrose diets of subjects with peripheral vascular disease significantly increases platelet adhesion.

57. High sugar consumption of pregnant adolescents can lead to substantial decrease in gestation duration and is associated with a twofold increased risk for delivering a small-for-gestational-age (SGA) infant.

58. Sugar is an addictive substance.

59. Sugar can be intoxicating, similar to alcohol.

60. Sugar given to premature babies can affect the amount of carbon dioxide they produce.

61. Decrease in sugar intake can increase emotional stability.

62. Your body changes sugar into 2 to 5 times more fat in the bloodstream than it does starch.

63. The rapid absorption of sugar promotes excessive food intake in obese subjects.

64. Sugar can worsen the symptoms of children with attention deficit hyperactivity disorder (ADHD).

65. Sugar adversely affects urinary electrolyte composition.

66. Sugar can slow down the ability of your adrenal glands to function.

67. Sugar has the potential of inducing abnormal metabolic processes in a normal healthy individual and to promote chronic degenerative diseases.

68. I.V.s (intravenous feedings) of sugar water can cut off oxygen to your brain.

69. Sugar increases your risk of polio.

70. High sugar intake can cause epileptic seizures.

71. Sugar causes high blood pressure in obese people.

72. In intensive care units: Limiting sugar saves lives.

73. Sugar may induce cell death.

74. In juvenile rehabilitation camps, when children were put on a low sugar diet, there was a 44 percent drop in antisocial behavior.

75. Sugar dehydrates newborns.

76. Sugar can cause gum disease.

Your body changes sugar into 2 to 5 times more fat in the bloodstream than it does starch.

High sugar intake can cause epileptic seizures.

I.V.s (intravenous feedings) of sugar water can cut off oxygen to your brain.

Refined Sugar — the Sweetest Poison of All...

Why Sugar Is Toxic To The Body

In 1957, Dr. William Coda Martin tried to answer the question: When is a food a food and when is it a poison? His working definition of "poison" was: "Medically: Any substance applied to the body, ingested or developed within the body, which causes or may cause disease. Physically: Any substance which inhibits the activity of a catalyst which is a minor substance, chemical or enzyme that activates a reaction." The dictionary gives an even broader definition for "poison": "to exert a harmful influence on, or to pervert".

Dr. Martin classified refined sugar as a poison because it has been depleted of its life forces, vitamins and minerals. "What is left consists of pure, refined carbohydrates. The body cannot utilize this refined starch and carbohydrate unless the depleted proteins, vitamins and minerals are present. Nature supplies these elements in each plant in quantities sufficient to metabolize the carbohydrate in that particular plant. There is no excess for other added carbohydrates. Incomplete

carbohydrate metabolism results in the formation of 'toxic metabolite' such as pyruvic acid and abnormal sugars containing five carbon atoms. Pyruvic acid accumulates in the brain and nervous system and the abnormal sugars in the red blood cells. These toxic metabolites interfere with the respiration of the cells. They cannot get sufficient oxygen to survive and function normally. In time, some of the cells die. This interferes with the function of a part of the body and is the beginning of degenerative disease."

Refined sugar is lethal when ingested by humans because it provides only that which nutritionists describe as "empty" or "naked" calories. It lacks the natural minerals which are present in the sugar beet or cane.

In addition, sugar is worse than nothing because it drains and leaches the body of precious vitamins and minerals through the demand its digestion, detoxification, and elimination makes upon one's entire system. So essential is balance to our bodies that we have many ways to provide against the sudden shock of a heavy intake of sugar. Minerals such as sodium (from salt),

Dr. Martin classified refined sugar as a poison because it has been depleted of its life forces, vitamins and minerals.

Refined sugar lacks the natural minerals which are present in the sugar beet or cane.

115

Excess sugar eventually affects every organ in the body.

When the liver is filled to its maximum capacity, the excess glycogen is returned to the blood in the form of fatty acids.

These fatty acids are taken to every part of the body and stored in the most inactive areas: the belly, the buttocks, the breasts and the thighs.

potassium, and magnesium (from vegetables), and calcium (from the bones) are mobilized and used in chemical transmutation; neutral acids are produced which attempt to return the acid-alkaline balance factor of the blood to a more normal state.

Sugar taken every day produces a continuously over acid condition, and more and more minerals are required from deep in the body in the attempt to rectify the imbalance. Finally, in order to protect the blood, so much calcium is taken from the bones and teeth that decay and general weakening begin. Excess sugar eventually affects every organ in the body. Initially, it is stored in the liver in the form of glucose (glycogen). Since the liver's capacity is limited, a daily intake of refined sugar (above the required amount of natural sugar) soon makes the liver expand like a balloon. When the liver is filled to its maximum capacity, the excess glycogen is returned to the blood in the form of fatty acids. These are taken to every part of the body and stored in the most inactive areas: the belly, the buttocks, the breasts and the thighs.

When these comparatively harmless places are completely filled, fatty acids are then distributed among active organs, such as the heart and kidneys. These begin to slow down; finally their tissues degenerate and turn to fat. The whole body is affected by their reduced ability, and abnormal blood pressure is created. The parasympathetic nervous system is affected; and organs governed by it, such as the small brain, become inactive or paralyzed. (Normal brain function is rarely thought of as being as biologic as digestion.) The circulatory and lymphatic systems are invaded, and the quality of the red corpuscles starts to change. An overabundance of white cells occurs, and the creation of tissue becomes slower. Our body's tolerance and immunizing power becomes more limited, so we cannot respond properly to extreme attacks, whether they be cold, heat, mosquitoes or microbes.

Excessive sugar has a strong mal-effect on the functioning of the brain. The key to orderly brain function is glutamic acid, a vital compound found in many vegetables. The B vitamins play a major role in dividing glutamic acid into antagonistic-complementary compounds which produce a "proceed" or "control" response in the brain. B vitamins are also manufactured by symbiotic bacteria which live in our intestines. When refined sugar is taken daily, these bacteria wither and die, and our stock of B vitamins gets very low. Too much sugar makes one sleepy; our ability to calculate and remember is lost.

SUCROSE: "Pure" Energy at a Price

When calories became the big thing in the 1920s, and everybody was learning to count them, the sugar pushers turned up with a new pitch. They boasted there were 2,500 calories in a pound of sugar. A little over a quarter-pound of sugar would produce 20 per cent of the total daily quota. "If you could buy all your food energy as cheaply as you buy calories in sugar," they told us, "your board bill for the year would be very low. If sugar were seven cents a pound, it would cost less than $35 for a whole year." A very inexpensive way to kill yourself. "Of course, we don't live on any such unbalanced diet," they admitted later. "But that figure serves to point out how inexpensive sugar is as an energy-building food. What was once a luxury only a privileged few could enjoy is now a food for the poorest of people."

Later, the sugar pushers advertised that sugar was chemically pure, topping Ivory soap in that department, being 99.9 per cent pure against Ivory's vaunted 99.44 per cent. "No food of our everyday diet is purer," we were assured. What was meant by purity, besides the unarguable fact that all vitamins, minerals, salts, fibers, and proteins had been removed in the refining process? Well, the sugar pushers came up with a new slant on purity. "You don't have to sort it like beans, wash it like rice. Every grain is like every other. No waste attends its use. No useless bones like in meat, no grounds like coffee."

"Pure" is a favorite adjective of the sugar pushers because it means one thing to the chemists and another thing to the ordinary mortals. When honey is labeled pure, this means that it is in its natural state (stolen directly from the bees who made it), with no adulteration with sucrose to stretch it and no harmful chemical residues which may have been sprayed on the flowers. It does not mean that the honey is free from minerals like iodine, iron, calcium, phosphorus, or multiple vitamins. So effective is the purification process which sugar cane and beets undergo in the refineries that sugar ends up as chemically pure as the morphine or the heroin a chemist has on the laboratory shelves.

What nutritional virtue this abstract chemical purity represents, the sugar pushers never tell us. Beginning with World War I, the sugar pushers coated their propaganda with a preparedness pitch. "Dietitians have known the high food value of sugar for a long time," said an industry tract of the 1920s. "But

Sugar was pushed as an inexpensive energy-building food. What was once a luxury only a privileged few could enjoy is now a food for the poorest of people.

Later, the sugar pushers advertised that sugar was chemically pure, topping Ivory soap in that department, being 99.9 per cent pure against Ivory's vaunted 99.44 per cent.

it took World War I to bring this home. The energy-building power of sugar reaches the muscles in minutes and it was of value to soldiers as a ration given them just before an attack was launched." The sugar pushers have been harping on the energy-building power of sucrose for years because it contains nothing else. Caloric energy and habit-forming taste: that's what sucrose has, and nothing else. All other foods contain energy plus. All foods contain some nutrients in the way of proteins, carbohydrates, vitamins or minerals, or all of these. Sucrose contains caloric energy, period.

The "quick" energy claim the sugar pushers talk about, which drives reluctant doughboys over the top and drives children up the wall, is based on the fact that refined sucrose is not digested in the mouth or the stomach but passes directly to the lower intestines and thence to the bloodstream. The extra speed with which sucrose enters the bloodstream does more harm than good. Much of the public confusion about refined sugar is compounded by language. Sugars are classified by chemists as "carbohydrates". This manufactured word means "a substance containing carbon with oxygen and hydrogen". If chemists want to use these hermetic terms in their laboratories when they talk to one another, fine. The use of the word "carbohydrate" outside the laboratory — especially in food labeling and advertising lingo — to describe both natural, complete cereal grains (which have been a principal food of mankind for thousands of years) and man-refined sugar (which is a manufactured drug and principal poison of mankind for only a few hundred years) is demonstrably wicked. This kind of confusion makes possible the flimflam practiced by sugar pushers to confound anxious mothers into thinking kiddies need sugar to survive.

The use of the word "carbohydrate" to describe sugar is deliberately misleading. Since the improved labeling of nutritional properties was required on packages and cans, refined carbohydrates like sugar are lumped together with those carbohydrates which may or may not be refined. The several types of carbohydrates are added together for an overall carbohydrate total. Thus, the effect of the label is to hide the sugar content from the unwary buyer. Chemists add to the confusion by using the word "sugar" to describe an entire group of substances that are similar but not identical. Glucose is a sugar found usually with other sugars, in fruits and vegetables. It is a key material in the metabolism of all plants and animals. Many of our principal foods are converted into glucose in our bodies. **Glucose** is always present in our bloodstream, and it is often called "blood sugar." **Dextrose**, also called "corn sugar", is derived synthetically from starch. **Fructose** is fruit sugar. **Maltose** is malt sugar. **Lactose** is milk sugar. **Sucrose is refined**

Caloric energy and habit-forming taste: that's what sucrose has, and nothing else.

Refined sucrose is not digested in the mouth or the stomach but passes directly to the lower intestines and thence to the bloodstream. The extra speed with which sucrose enters the bloodstream does more harm than good.

sugar made from sugar cane and sugar beet. Glucose has always been an essential element in the human bloodstream. Sucrose addiction is something new in the history of the human animal.

To use the word "sugar" to describe two substances which are far from being identical, which have different chemical structures and which affect the body in profoundly different ways compounds confusion. It makes possible more flimflam from the sugar pushers who tell us how important sugar is as an essential component of the human body, how it is oxidized to produce energy, how it is metabolized to produce warmth, and so on. They're talking about glucose, of course, which is manufactured in our bodies. However, one is led to believe that the manufacturers are talking about the sucrose which is made in their refineries. When the word "sugar" can mean the glucose in your blood as well as the sucrose in your Coca-Cola, it's great for the sugar pushers but it's rough on everybody else.

People have been bamboozled into thinking of their bodies the way they think of their checking accounts. If they suspect they have low blood sugar, they are programmed to snack on vending machine candies and sodas in order to raise their blood sugar level. Actually, this is the worst thing to do. The level of glucose in their blood is apt to be low because they are addicted to sucrose. People who kick sucrose addiction and stay off sucrose find that the glucose level of their blood returns to normal and stays there. Since the late 1960s, millions of Americans have returned to natural food. A new type of store, the natural food store, has encouraged many to become dropouts from the supermarket. Natural food can be instrumental in restoring health. Many people, therefore, have come to equate the word "natural" with "healthy".

So the sugar pushers have begun to pervert the word "natural" in order to mislead the public. "Made from natural ingredients", the television sugar-pushers tell us about product after product. The word "from" is not accented on television. It should be. Even refined sugar is made from natural ingredients. There is nothing new about that. The natural ingredients are cane and beets. But that four-letter word "from" hardly suggests that 90 per cent of the cane and beet have been removed. Heroin, too, could be advertised as being made from natural ingredients. The opium poppy is as natural as the sugar beet. It's what man does with it that tells the story. If you want to avoid sugar in the supermarket, there is only one sure way. Don't buy anything unless it says on the label prominently, in plain English: "No sugar added". Use of the word "carbohydrate" as a "scientific" word for sugar has become a standard defense strategy with sugar pushers and many of their medical apologists. It's their security blanket.

Glucose has always been an essential element in the human bloodstream.

When the word "sugar" can mean the glucose in your blood as well as the sucrose in your Coca-Cola, it's great for the sugar pushers but it's rough on everybody else.

So the sugar pushers have begun to pervert the word "natural" in order to mislead the public.

119

Sugar and Mental Health

In the Dark Ages, troubled souls were rarely locked up for going off their rocker. Such confinement began in the Age of Enlightenment, after sugar made the transition from apothecary's prescription to candymaker's confection. "The great confinement of the insane", as one historian calls it, began in the late 17th century, after sugar consumption in Britain had zoomed in 200 years from a pinch or two in a barrel of beer, here and there, to more than two million pounds per year. By that time, physicians in London had begun to observe and record terminal physical signs and symptoms of the "sugar blues".

Meanwhile, when sugar eaters did not manifest obvious terminal physical symptoms and the physicians were professionally bewildered, patients were no longer pronounced bewitched, but mad, insane, emotionally disturbed. Laziness, fatigue, debauchery, parental displeasure — any one problem was sufficient cause for people under twenty-five to be locked up in the first Parisian mental hospitals. All it took to be incarcerated was a complaint from parents, relatives, or the omnipotent parish priest. Wet nurses with their babies, pregnant youngsters, retarded or defective children, senior citizens, paralytics, epileptics, prostitutes, or raving lunatics — anyone wanted off the streets and out of sight was put away. The mental hospital succeeded witch-hunting and heresy-hounding as a more enlightened and humane method of social control. The physician and priest handled the dirty work of street sweeping in return for royal favors.

Initially, when the General Hospital was established in Paris by royal decree, one per cent of the city's population was locked up. From that time until the 20 century, as the consumption of sugar went up and up — especially in the cities — so did the number of people who were put away in the General Hospital. Three hundred years later, the "emotionally disturbed" can be turned into walking automatons, their brains controlled with psychoactive drugs. Today, pioneers of orthomolecular psychiatry, such as Dr. Abram Hoffer, Dr. Allan Cott, Dr. A. Cherkin as well as Dr. Linus Pauling, have confirmed that mental illness is a myth and that emotional disturbance can be merely the first symptom of the obvious inability of the human system to handle the stress of sugar dependency. In Orthomolecular Psychiatry, Dr. Pauling writes: "The functioning of

From that time until the 20 century, as the consumption of sugar went up and up—especially in the cities—so did the number of people who were put away in the General Hospital.

Today, pioneers of orthomolecular psychiatry have confirmed that mental illness is a myth and that emotional disturbance can be merely the first symptom of the obvious inability of the human system to handle the stress of sugar dependency.

the brain and nervous tissue is more sensitively dependent on the rate of chemical reactions than the functioning of other organs and tissues. I believe that mental disease is for the most part caused by abnormal reaction rates, as determined by genetic constitution and diet, and by abnormal molecular concentrations of essential substances. Selection of food (and drugs) in a world that is undergoing rapid scientific and technological change may often be far from the best."

In Megavitamin B3 Therapy for Schizophrenia, Dr. Abram Hoffer notes: "Patients are also advised to follow a good nutritional program with restriction of sucrose and sucrose-rich foods." Clinical research with hyperactive and psychotic children, as well as those with brain injuries and learning disabilities, has shown: "An abnormally high family history of diabetes — that is, parents and grandparents who cannot handle sugar; an abnormally high incidence of low blood glucose, or functional hypoglycemia in the children themselves, which indicates that their systems cannot handle sugar; dependence on a high level of sugar in the diets of the very children who cannot handle it." Inquiry into the dietary history of patients diagnosed as schizophrenic reveals the diet of their choice is rich in sweets, candy, cakes, coffee, caffeinated beverages, and foods prepared with sugar. These foods, which stimulate the adrenals, should be eliminated or severely restricted."

The avant-garde of modern medicine has rediscovered what the lowly sorceress learned long ago through painstaking study of nature. "In more than twenty years of psychiatric work," writes DR Thomas Szasz, "I have never known a clinical psychologist to report, on the basis of a projective test, that the subject is a normal, mentally healthy person. While some witches may have survived dunking, no 'madman' survives psychological testing... there is no behavior or person that a modern psychiatrist cannot plausibly diagnose as abnormal or ill." So it was in the 17th century. Once the doctor or the exorcist had been called in, he was under pressure to do something. When he tried and failed, the poor patient had to be put away. It is often said that surgeons bury their mistakes. Physicians and psychiatrists put them away; lock 'em up.

In the 1940s, DR John Tintera rediscovered the vital importance of the endocrine system, especially the adrenal glands, in "pathological mentation" or "brain boggling." In 200 cases under treatment for hypoadrenocorticism (the lack of adequate adrenal cortical hormone production or imbalance among these hormones), he discovered that the chief complaints of his patients were often similar to those found in persons whose systems were unable to handle sugar: fatigue, nervousness, depression, apprehension, craving for sweets, inability to handle alcohol, inability to concentrate, allergies, low blood pressure. Sugar blues!

DR Tintera finally insisted that all his patients submit to a four-hour glucose tolerance test (GTT) to find out whether or not they could handle sugar. The results were so startling that the laboratories double-checked their techniques, then apologized for what they believed to be incorrect readings. What mystified them was the low, flat curves derived from disturbed, early adolescents. This laboratory procedure had been previously carried out only for patients with physical findings presumptive of diabetes. Dorland's definition of schizophrenia (Bleuler's dementia praecox) includes the phrase, "often recognized during or shortly after adolescence", and further, in reference to hebephrenia and catatonia, "coming on soon after the onset of puberty". These conditions might seem to arise or become aggravated at puberty, but probing into the patient's past will frequently reveal indications which were present at birth, during the first year of life, and through the preschool and grammar school years. Each of these periods has its own characteristic clinical picture.

This picture becomes more marked at pubescence and often causes school officials to complain of juvenile delinquency or underachievement. A glucose tolerance test at any of these periods could alert parents and physicians and could save innumerable hours and small fortunes spent in looking into the child's psyche and home environment for maladjustments of questionable significance in the emotional development of the average child. The negativism, hyperactivity and obstinate resentment of discipline are absolute indications for at least the minimum laboratory tests: urinalysis, complete blood count, PBI determination, and the five-hour glucose tolerance test. A GTT can be performed on a young child by the micro-method without undue trauma to the patient. As a matter of fact, I have been urging that these four tests be routine for all patients, even before a history or physical examination is undertaken. In almost all discussions on drug addiction, alcoholism and schizophrenia, it is claimed that there is no definite constitutional type that falls prey to these afflictions.

Almost universally, the statement is made that all of these individuals are emotionally immature. It has long been our goal

The negativism, hyperactivity and obstinate resentment of discipline are absolute indications for at least the minimum laboratory tests: urinalysis, complete blood count, PBI determination, and the five-hour glucose tolerance test.

123

Tintera said over and over again that "the importance of diet cannot be overemphasized". He laid out a sweeping permanent injunction against sugar in all forms and guises.

Nobody, but nobody, should ever be allowed to begin what is called "psychiatric treatment", anyplace, anywhere, unless and until they have had a glucose tolerance test to discover if they can handle sugar.

to persuade every physician, whether oriented toward psychiatry, genetics or physiology, to recognize that one type of endocrine individual is involved in the majority of these cases: the hypoadrenocortic. Tintera published several epochal medical papers. Over and over, he emphasized that improvement, alleviation, palliation or cure was "dependent upon the restoration of the normal function of the total organism". His first prescribed item of treatment was diet. Over and over again, he said that "the importance of diet cannot be overemphasized". He laid out a sweeping permanent injunction against sugar in all forms and guises.

While Egas Moniz of Portugal was receiving a Nobel Prize for devising the lobotomy operation for the treatment of schizophrenia, Tintera's reward was to be harassment and hounding by the pundits of organized medicine. While Tintera's sweeping implication of sugar as a cause of what was called "schizophrenia" could be confined to medical journals, he was let alone, ignored. He could be tolerated if he stayed in his assigned territory, endocrinology. Even when he suggested that alcoholism was related to adrenals that had been whipped by sugar abuse, they let him alone; because the medicos had decided there was nothing in alcoholism for them except aggravation, they were

satisfied to abandon it to Alcoholics Anonymous.

However, when Tintera dared to suggest in a magazine of general circulation that "it is ridiculous to talk of kinds of allergies when there is only one kind, which is adrenal glands impaired... by sugar", he could no longer be ignored. The allergists had a great racket going for themselves. Allergic souls had been entertaining each other for years with tall tales of exotic allergies — everything from horse feathers to lobster tails. Along comes someone who says none of this matters: take them off sugar and keep them off it.

Perhaps Tintera's untimely death in 1969 at the age of fifty-seven made it easier for the medical profession to accept discoveries that had once seemed as far out as the simple oriental medical thesis of genetics and diet, yin and yang. Today, doctors all over the world are repeating what Tintera announced years ago: nobody, but nobody, should ever be allowed to begin what is called "psychiatric treatment", anyplace, anywhere, unless and until they have had a glucose tolerance test to discover if they can handle sugar. So called preventive medicine goes further and suggests that since we only think we can handle sugar because we initially have strong adrenals, why wait until they give us signs and signals that they're worn out?

124

Take the load off now by eliminating sugar in all forms and guises, starting with that soda pop you have in your hand. The mind truly boggles when one glances over what passes for medical history. Through the centuries, troubled souls have been barbecued for bewitchment, exorcised for possession, locked up for insanity, tortured for masturbatory madness, psychiatrised for psychosis, lobotomised for schizophrenia. How many patients would have listened if the local healer had told them that the only thing ailing them was *sugar blues*?

How many patients would have listened if the local healer had told them that the only thing ailing them was sugar blues?

Sugar and Cancer

Of the over 4 million cancer patients being treated in the U.S. today, almost none are offered any scientifically guided nutrition therapy other than being told to "just eat good foods." Many cancer patients would have a major improvement in their conditions if they controlled the supply of cancer's preferred fuel: GLUCOSE. By slowing the cancer's growth, patients make it possible for their immune systems to catch up to the disease. Controlling one's blood-glucose levels through diet, exercise, supplements, meditation and prescription drugs — when necessary — can be one of the most crucial components to a cancer treatment program. The saying "Sugar feeds cancer" is simple. The explanation is a little more involved.

German Otto Warburg, Ph.D., the 1931 Nobel laureate in medicine, first discovered that cancer cells have a fundamentally different energy metabolism compared to healthy cells.

The gist of his Nobel thesis was this: Malignant tumors frequently exhibit an increase in "anaerobic glycolysis" — a process whereby glucose is used by cancer cells as a fuel with lactic acid as an anaerobic by-product — compared to normal tissues.

The large amount of lactic acid produced by this fermentation of glucose from the cancer cells is then transported to the liver. This conversion of glucose to lactate creates a lower, more acidic pH in cancerous tissues as well as overall physical fatigue from lactic acid build-up. Therefore, larger tumors tend to exhibit a more acidic pH.

Hence, cancer therapies should attempt to regulate blood-glucose levels through diet, supplements, exercise, medication when necessary, gradual weight loss, and stress reduction. Since cancer cells derive most of their energy from anaerobic glycolysis, the goal is not to eliminate sugars or carbohydrates entirely from the diet but rather to control blood-glucose within a narrow range to help starve the cancer cells and boost immune function.

> Many cancer patients would have a major improvement in their conditions if they controlled the supply of cancer's preferred fuel: GLUCOSE.

Can Sugar Worsen Cholesterol?

Researchers have found a link between sugar and unhealthy levels of blood fats. "There's an association between added sugar intake and what we call dyslipidemia — higher triglycerides and lower HDL ("good") cholesterol, says Rachel K. Johnson, RD, MPH, PhD, a professor of nutrition at the University of Vermont and a spokeswoman for the American Heart Association (AHA).

In a study recently published in the *Journal of the American Medical Association* (JAMA), people who ate the largest amounts of added sugar had the highest blood triglyceride levels and the lowest HDL (good) cholesterol levels. That study also showed that eating lots of sugar more than tripled the odds of having low HDL cholesterol levels, a strong risk factor for heart disease.

In contrast, people who ate the least sugar had the lowest triglyceride levels and highest HDL levels, a protective factor against heart disease.

But "the study doesn't prove that added sugars cause dyslipidemia," says Johnson, who wasn't involved in the JAMA study.

Johnson says that to prove that sugar causes problems with blood fats, scientists would have to conduct a clinical trial in which some people ate a diet high in added sugar and others ate a diet low in added sugar. Then researchers would track their triglyceride and cholesterol levels. Such a study would be expensive and hard to carry out, she says.

However, Johnson points out that weight did not explain the JAMA findings. "Obesity is obviously related to dyslipidemia, but based on the JAMA paper, the added sugars had an independent effect, separate and distinct from the added sugars' impact on weight," she says.

In a recently published study, people who ate the largest amounts of added sugar had the highest blood triglyceride levels and the lowest HDL (good) cholesterol levels.

Correct Food Combining

Whether it's sugared cereal or pastry and black coffee for breakfast, whether it's hamburgers and Coca-Cola for lunch or the full "gourmet" dinner in the evening, chemically the average American diet is a formula that guarantees bubble, bubble, stomach trouble. Unless you've taken too much insulin and, in a state of insulin shock, need sugar as an antidote, hardly anyone ever has cause to take sugar alone. Humans need sugar as much as they need the nicotine in tobacco. Crave it is one thing — need it is another. From the days of the Persian Empire to our own, sugar has usually been used to hop up the flavor of other food and drink, as an ingredient in the kitchen or as a condiment at the table. Let us leave aside for the moment the known effect of sugar (long-term and short-term) on the entire system and concentrate on the effect of sugar taken in combination with other daily foods.

When Grandma warned that sugared cookies before meals "will spoil your supper," she knew what she was talking about. Her explanation might not have satisfied a chemist but, as with many traditional axioms from the Mosaic law on kosher food and separation in the kitchen, such rules are based on years of trial and error and are apt to be right on the button. Most modern research in combining food is a labored discovery of the things Grandma took for granted. Any diet or regimen undertaken for the single purpose of losing weight is dangerous, by definition. Obesity is talked about and treated as a disease in 20th century America. Obesity is not a disease. It is only a symptom, a sign, a warning that your body is out of order. Dieting to lose weight is as silly and dangerous as taking aspirin to relieve a headache before you know the reason for the headache.

Getting rid of a symptom is like turning off an alarm. It leaves the basic cause untouched. Any diet or regimen undertaken with any objective short of restoration of total health of your body is dangerous. Many overweight people are undernourished. (Dr. H. Curtis Wood stresses this point in his 1971 book, *Overfed But Undernourished*.) Eating less can aggravate this condition, unless one is concerned with the quality of the food instead of just its quantity. Many people — doctors included — assume that if weight is lost, fat is lost. This is not necessarily so. Any diet which lumps all carbohydrates together is dangerous. Any diet which does not consider the quality of carbohydrates and makes the crucial life-and-death distinction

Chemically the average American diet is a formula that guarantees bubble, bubble, stomach trouble.

Obesity is not a disease. It is only a symptom, a sign, a warning that your body is out of order.

Many overweight people are undernourished.

131

between natural, unrefined carbohydrates like whole grains and vegetables and man-refined carbohydrates like sugar and white flour is dangerous. Any diet which includes refined sugar and white flour, no matter what "scientific" name is applied to them, is dangerous.

Kicking sugar and white flour and substituting whole grains, vegetables and natural fruits in season, is the core of any sensible natural regimen. Changing the quality of your carbohydrates can change the quality of your health and life. If you eat natural food of good quality, quantity tends to take care of itself. Nobody is going to eat a half-dozen sugar beets or a whole case of sugar cane. Even if they do, it will be less dangerous than a few ounces of sugar. Sugar of all kinds — natural sugars, such as those in honey and fruit (fructose), as well as the refined white stuff (sucrose) — tends to arrest the secretion of gastric juices and have an inhibiting effect on the stomach's natural ability to move. Sugars are not digested in the mouth, like cereals, or in the stomach, like animal flesh. When taken alone, they pass quickly through the stomach into the small intestine. When sugars are eaten with other foods — perhaps meat and bread in a sandwich — they are held up in the stomach for a while.

The sugar in the bread and the Coke sit there with the hamburger and the bun waiting for them to be digested. While the stomach is working on the animal protein and the refined starch in the bread, the addition of the sugar practically guarantees rapid acid fermentation under the conditions of warmth and moisture existing in the stomach. One lump of sugar in your coffee after a sandwich is enough to turn your stomach into a fermenter. One soda with a hamburger is enough to turn your stomach into a still. Sugar on cereal — whether you buy it already sugared in a box or add it yourself — almost guarantees acid fermentation.

Since the beginning of time, natural laws were observed, in both senses of that word, when it came to eating foods in combination. Birds have been observed eating insects at one period in the day and seeds at another. Other animals tend to eat one food at a time. Flesh-eating animals take their protein raw and straight. In the Orient, it is traditional to eat yang before yin. Miso soup (fermented soybean protein, yang) for breakfast; raw fish (more yang protein) at the beginning of the meal; afterwards comes the rice (which is less yang than the miso and fish); and then the vegetables which are yin. If you ever eat with a traditional Japanese family and you violate this order, the Orientals (if your friends) will correct you courteously but firmly. The law observed by Orthodox Jews prohibits many combinations at the same meal,

> Any diet which includes refined sugar and white flour, no matter what "scientific" name is applied to them, is dangerous.

> One lump of sugar in your coffee after a sandwich is enough to turn your stomach into a fermenter. One soda with a hamburger is enough to turn your stomach into a still.

especially flesh and dairy products. Special utensils for the dairy meal and different utensils for the flesh meal reinforce that taboo at the food's source in the kitchen.

Man learned very early in the game what improper combinations of food could do to the human system. When he got a stomach ache from combining raw fruit with grain, or honey with porridge, he didn't reach for an antacid tablet. He learned not to eat that way. When gluttony and excess became widespread, religious codes and commandments were invoked against it. Gluttony is a capital sin in most religions; but there are no specific religious warnings or commandments against refined sugar because sugar abuse — like drug abuse — did not appear on the world scene until centuries after holy books had gone to press.

"Why must we accept as normal what we find in a race of sick and weakened human beings?" Dr. Herbert M. Shelton asks. "Must we always take it for granted that the present eating practices of civilized men are normal? Foul stools, loose stools, impacted stools, pebbly stools, much foul gas, colitis, hemorrhoids, bleeding with stools, the need for toilet paper are swept into the orbit of the normal."

When starches and complex sugars (like those in honey and fruits) are digested, they are broken down into simple sugars called "monosaccharides", which are usable substances — nutriments. When starches and sugars are taken together and undergo fermentation, they are broken down into carbon dioxide, acetic acid, alcohol, and water. With the exception of the water, all these are unusable substances — poisons. When proteins are digested, they are broken down into amino acids, which are usable substances — nutriments. When proteins are taken with sugar, they putrefy; they are broken down into a variety of ptomaines and leucomaines, which are nonusable substances — poisons. Enzymic digestion of foods prepares them for use by our body. Bacterial decomposition makes them unfit for use by our body. The first process gives us nutriments; the second gives us poisons.

Much that passes for modern nutrition is obsessed with a mania for quantitative counting. The body is treated like a checking account. Deposit calories (like dollars) and withdraw energy. Deposit proteins, carbohydrates, fats, vitamins, and minerals — balanced quantitatively — and the result, theoretically, is a healthy body. People qualify as healthy today if they can crawl out of bed, get to the office and sign in. If they can't make it, call the doctor to qualify for sick pay, hospitalization, rest cure — anything from a day's pay without working to an artificial kidney, courtesy of the taxpayers.

When proteins are taken with sugar, they putrefy; they are broken down into a variety of ptomaines and leucomaines, which are nonusable substances — poisons.

133

"To derive sustenance from foods eaten, they must be digested," Shelton warned years ago. "They must not rot."

But what does it profit someone if the theoretically required calories and nutrients are consumed daily, yet this random eat-on-the-run, snack-time collection of foods ferments and putrefies in the digestive tract? What good is it if the body is fed protein, only to have it putrefy in the gastrointestinal canal? Carbohydrates that ferment in the digestive tract are converted into alcohol and acetic acid, not digestible monosaccharides. "To derive sustenance from foods eaten, they must be digested," Shelton warned years ago. "They must not rot." Sure, the body can get rid of poisons through the urine and the pores; the amount of poisons in the urine is taken as an index to what's going on in the intestine. The body does establish a tolerance for these poisons, just as it adjusts gradually to an intake of heroin. But, says Shelton, "the discomfort from accumulation of gas, the bad breath, and foul and unpleasant odors are as undesirable as are the poisons."

The Dangers of Aspartame

You may be sick and don't even know it?

There are 92 documented symptoms of ASPARTAME, from coma to death. The majority of them are all neurological because the ASPARTAME destroys the nervous system.

ASPARTAME Disease is partially the cause to what is behind some of the mystery of the Dessert Storm health problems some of the soldiers are experiencing. The burning tongue and other problems discussed in over 60 cases can be directly related to the consumption of an *ASPARTAME* product. Several thousand pallets of diet pop were shipped to the Dessert Storm troops. (Heat can liberate the methanol from the ASPARTAME at 86 degrees F). Diet pop sat in the 120 degree F. Arabian sun for weeks at a time on pallets. The service men and women drank this diet pop all day long. All of their symptoms are identical to ASPARTAME poisoning.

You may have never known that aspartame can poison. This is in no small part because the diet industry is worth a ton of money to some big name companies, and they want to protect their income even if it means your health! When NutraSweet came to market for the second time in 1981, a new diet craze was born and low carb was the rage. The money started to pour in for artificial sweeteners and there was a niche market ready to be marketed to.

The 1976 Groliers encyclopedia states cancer cannot live without phenylalanine. Aspartame is 50% phenylalanine.

Many people have reported the following side effects from aspartame:

- Fibromyalgia Syndrome and symptoms of Fibromyalgia
- Multiple Sclerosis symptoms
- Dizziness
- Headaches
- Menstrual problems
- Behavioral changes observed after intake of aspartame flavored foods and drinks are moodiness, nausea, hallucinations, seizures, twitching, abnormal breathing, and depression.

How does this happen? When Aspartame is synthesized from the amino acids, Phenylalanine, and Aspartic Acid, in the presence of methyl alcohol, amino acid imbalances immediately result

ASPARTAME destroys the nervous system.

You may have never known that aspartame can poison. This is in no small part because the diet industry is worth a ton of money to some big name companies, and they want to protect their income even if it means your health!

causing interruption of the normal neurotransmitter metabolism of the human brain.

The amino acid neurotransmitter Tryptophan is less available for its known action for optimal brain serotonin levels. This in turn arouses systemic hypertension, insomnia, hyperactivity, general contraindication to those taking the medications levodopa or monoamine oxidase inhibitors.

The structure of aspartame seems simple, but what a complicated structure aspartame really is. Two isolated amino acids in aspartame are fused together by its third component, deadly methanol. In this structure, methanol bonds the two amino acids together, but when released at a mere 86 degrees Fahrenheit, the methanol becomes a poisonous free radical.

Methanol breaks down into formic acid and formaldehyde, embalming fluid. Methanol is a dangerous neurotoxin, a known carcinogen, causes retinal damage in the eye, interferes with DNA replication, and causes birth defects. Aspartame can be found on the ingredients list in the following products:

Diet pop, over-the-counter drugs and prescription drugs (very common and listed under "inactive ingredients"), vitamin and herb supplements, yogurt, instant breakfasts, candy, breath mints, cereals, sugar-free chewing gum, cocoa mixes, coffee beverages, instant breakfasts, gelatin desserts, frozen desserts, juice beverages, laxatives, milk drinks, shake mixes, tabletop sweeteners, tea beverages, instant teas and coffees, topping mixes, wine coolers, etc.

Also, some drug and supplement manufacturers are allowed to avoid listing aspartame on the label if they state the words, "contains phenylalanine."

Why Diet Pop and Colas make you fat and sick.

Many times people come in to train with me and ask what can I do to lose weight? One of the very first questions I ask is — Do you drink diet pop?

Effective weight loss starts with diet changes and exercise, one of the first changes is to stop drinking all diet pop, all colas, all carbonated beverages — including diet pop, which is the worst. Get the Aspartame out of your diet!

Why? Diet pop is very acidic, with a pH of 1.5 to 2.5 — that is 100,000 times more acid that your body wants to be. **Aspartame has a pH of 1.5!** All life dies at a pH of 4.5.

Because of this your body

Two isolated amino acids in aspartame are fused together by its third component, deadly methanol.

Methanol breaks down into formic acid and formaldehyde, embalming fluid.

Some drug and supplement manufacturers are allowed to avoid listing aspartame on the label if they state the words, "contains phenylalanine."

136

creates fat cells to store the extra acid or in this case Aspartame. This is why people who drink diet pop just get fatter.

Your kidneys are the prime pH balancing organs in your body. The body wants to have a general pH of about 7. So when you drink pure water with pH of about 7 or a little higher — you are balancing the pH in your kidneys, and balancing the general pH in the body. When the pH is right the body can release and dispose of stored acids, which are filling the fat cells. This why some clients have had such drastic weight reductions in such a short amount of time, just drink water.

Why is pH so important? If your pH is correct you will have a much less chance of contracting a chronic condition, such as cancer, arthritis, or even the common cold.

There is a direct correlation between pH and your immune system. The Immune system works at its most optimal level when the body pH is 7.0 — or slightly alkaline.

So when you drink just one diet pop — you drive your pH down, shutting down the immune system, and setting yourself up for a disease to take hold. **Drink just one diet pop or cola, you will then have to drink 32 glasses of water with a pH of 7 or more to balance your pH .**

Scientists have found that

healthy people have body fluids that are slightly alkaline, 7.1 to 7.5 pH. Scientists and doctors have also found that over 150 degenerative diseases are linked to acidity, including cancer, diabetes, arthritis, heart disease, gall and kidney stones, and many more. All diseases thrive in an acidic, oxygen poor environment.

Keep in mind that a drop in every point on the pH scale is 10x more acidic than the previous number — i.e. from 7 to 6 is 10x, from 7 to 5 is 100x etc. From 7 to 2 is 100,000x more acidic, colas are in the approximate 2.5 pH range. **Almost no soda(pop) is higher than 3.0.** Diet sodas are the worst as they have the highest acid content. Actually diet sodas cause you to gain weight because they alter the blood chemistry, making changes in your metabolism, leading to a slower metabolic rate. The best liquid to drink is water.

Most degenerative diseases we call "Old-Age Diseases" like memory loss, osteoporosis, arthritis, diabetes, hypertension, and many more are actually life style diseases caused by acidosis, the lack of supplements, what acids we ingest, what nutrients we don't ingest, or toxins we don't properly eliminate.

When the temperature of ASPARTAME exceeds 86 degrees F, the wood alcohol in ASPARTAME

Aspartame has a pH of 1.5! All life dies at a pH of 4.5.

The Immune system works at its most optimal level, when the body pH is 7.0 — or slightly alkaline.

Old-Age Diseases" like memory loss, osteoporosis, arthritis, diabetes, hypertension, and many more are actually life style diseases caused by acidosis, the lack of supplements, what acids we ingest, what nutrients we don't ingest, or toxins we don't properly eliminate.

coverts to formaldehyde and then to formic acid, which in turn causes metabolic acidosis. (Formic acid is the poison found in the sting of fire ants). The methanol toxicity mimics multiple sclerosis; thus people were being diagnosed with having multiple sclerosis in error. The multiple sclerosis is not a death sentence, where methanol toxicity is. In the case of systemic lupus, we are finding it has become almost as rampant as multiple sclerosis, especially with Diet Coke and Diet Pepsi drinkers. Also, with methanol toxicity, the victims usually drink three to four 12 oz. cans of them per day, some even more.

On the other hand, in the case of those diagnosed with Multiple Sclerosis, (when in reality, the disease is methanol toxicity), most of the symptoms disappear. We have seen cases where their vision has returned and even their hearing has returned. This also applies to cases of tinnitus. If you are using ASPARTAME (NutraSweet, Equal, Spoonful, etc.) and you suffer from fibromyalgia symptoms, spasms, shooting pains, numbness in your legs, cramps, vertigo, dizziness, headaches, tinnitus, joint pain, depression, anxiety attacks, slurred speech, blurred vision, or memory loss-you probably have
ASPARTAME DISEASE!

ASPARTAME changes the brain's chemistry. It is the reason for severe seizures. This drug changes the dopamine level in the brain. Imagine what this drug does to patients suffering from Parkinson's Disease. This drug also causes Birth Defects. There is absolutely no reason to take this product. It is NOT A DIET PRODUCT!!! The Congressional record said, "It makes you crave carbohydrates and will make you FAT." Dr. Roberts stated that when he got patients off ASPARTAME, their average weight loss was 19 pounds per person. The formaldehyde stores in the fat cells, particularly in the hips and thighs.

According to the Conference of the American College of Physicians, "We are talking about a plague of neurological diseases caused by this deadly poison". Dr. Roberts realized what was happening when ASPARTAME was first marketed. He said "his diabetic patients presented memory loss, confusion, and severe vision loss". At the Conference of the American College of Physicians, doctors admitted that they did not know. They had wondered why seizures were rampant (the phenylalanine in ASPARTAME breaks down the seizure threshold and depletes serotonin, which causes manic depression, panic attacks, rage, and violence).

I assure you that MONSANTO, the creator of ASPARTAME, knows the dangers. They fund the American Diabetes Association,

American Dietetic Association, Congress, and the Conference of the American College of Physicians. The New York Times, on November 15, 1996, ran an article on how the American Dietetic Association takes money from the food industry to endorse their products. Therefore, they can not criticize any additives or tell about their link to MONSANTO.

Dr. Roberts says "consuming ASPARTAME at the time of conception can cause birth defects". The phenylalanine concentrates in the placenta, causing mental retardation, according to Dr. Louis Elsas, Pediatrician Professor of Genetics, at Emory University in his testimony before Congress.

What Is Aspartame Made Of?

1. Aspartic Acid (40 percent of Aspartame)

Dr. Russell L. Blaylock, a professor of neurosurgery at the Medical University of Mississippi, recently published a book thoroughly detailing the damage that is caused by the ingestion of excessive aspartic acid from aspartame. Blaylock makes use of almost 500 scientific references to show how excess free excitatory amino acids such as aspartic acid and glutamic acid (about 99 percent of monosodium glutamate (MSG) is glutamic acid) in our food supply are causing serious chronic neurological disorders and a myriad of other acute symptoms.

How Aspartate (and Glutamate) Cause Damage

Aspartate and glutamate act as neurotransmitters in the brain by facilitating the transmission of information from neuron to neuron. Too much aspartate or glutamate in the brain kills certain neurons by allowing the influx of too much calcium into the cells. This influx triggers excessive amounts of free radicals, which kill the cells. The neural cell damage that can be caused by excessive aspartate and glutamate is why they are referred to as "excitotoxins." They "excite" or stimulate the neural cells to death.

Aspartic acid is an amino acid. Taken in its free form (unbound to proteins) it significantly raises the blood plasma level of aspartate and glutamate. The excess aspartate and glutamate in the blood plasma shortly after ingesting aspartame or products with free glutamic acid (glutamate precursor) leads to a high level of those neurotransmitters in certain areas of the brain.

The blood brain barrier (BBB), which normally protects the brain from excess glutamate and aspartate as well as toxins:

1. Is not fully developed during childhood...

2. Does not fully protect all areas of the brain

3. Is damaged by numerous chronic and acute conditions, and...

4. Allows seepage of excess glutamate and aspartate into the brain even when intact.

The excess glutamate and aspartate slowly begin to destroy neurons. The large majority (75 percent or more) of neural cells in a particular area of the brain are killed before any clinical symptoms of a chronic illness are noticed. A few of the many chronic illnesses that have been shown to be contributed to by long-term exposure to excitatory amino acid damage include:

• Multiple sclerosis (MS)

• ALS

• Memory loss

• Hormonal problems

• Hearing loss

• Epilepsy

• Alzheimer's disease

• Parkinson's disease

• Hypoglycemia

• AIDS

• Dementia

• Brain lesions

• Neuroendocrine disorders

The risk to infants, children, pregnant women, the elderly, and persons with certain chronic health problems from excitotoxins are great. Even the Federation of American Societies for Experimental Biology (FASEB), which usually understates problems and mimics the FDA party-line, recently stated in a review that:

"It is prudent to avoid the use of dietary supplements of L-glutamic acid by pregnant women, infants, and children. The existence of evidence of potential endocrine responses, i.e., elevated cortisol and prolactin, and differential responses between males and females, would also suggest a neuroendocrine link and that supplemental L-glutamic acid should be avoided by women of childbearing age and individuals with affective disorders."

Aspartic acid from aspartame has the same deleterious effects on the body as glutamic acid. The exact mechanism of acute reactions to excess free glutamate and aspartate is currently being debated. As reported to the FDA, those reactions include:

• Headaches/migraines

• Nausea

• Abdominal pains

• Fatigue (blocks sufficient

glucose entry into brain)

- Sleep problems
- Vision problems
- Anxiety attacks
- Depression
- Asthma/chest tightness.

One common complaint of persons suffering from the effect of aspartame is memory loss. Ironically, in 1987, G.D. Searle, the manufacturer of aspartame, undertook a search for a drug to combat memory loss caused by excitatory amino acid damage. Blaylock is one of many scientists and physicians who are concerned about excitatory amino acid damage caused by ingestion of aspartame and MSG.

A few of the many experts who have spoken out against the damage being caused by aspartate and glutamate include Adrienne Samuels, Ph.D., an experimental psychologist specializing in research design. Another is Olney, a professor in the department of psychiatry, School of Medicine, Washington University, a neuroscientist and researcher, and one of the world's foremost authorities on excitotoxins. (He informed Searle in 1971 that aspartic acid caused holes in the brains of mice.)

2. Phenylalanine (50 percent of aspartame)

Phenylalanine is an amino acid

normally found in the brain. Persons with the genetic disorder phenylketonuria (PKU) cannot metabolize phenylalanine. This leads to dangerously high levels of phenylalanine in the brain (sometimes lethal). It has been shown that ingesting aspartame, especially along with carbohydrates, can lead to excess levels of phenylalanine in the brain even in persons who do not have PKU.

This is not just a theory, as many people who have eaten large amounts of aspartame over a long period of time and do not have PKU have been shown to have excessive levels of phenylalanine in the blood. Excessive levels of phenylalanine in the brain can cause the levels of serotonin in the brain to decrease, leading to emotional disorders such as depression. It was shown in human testing that phenylalanine levels of the blood were increased significantly in human subjects who chronically used aspartame.

Even a single use of aspartame raised the blood phenylalanine levels. In his testimony before the U.S. Congress, Dr. Louis J. Elsas showed that high blood phenylalanine can be concentrated in parts of the brain and is especially dangerous for infants and fetuses. He also showed that phenylalanine is metabolized much more efficiently by rodents than by humans.

One common complaint of persons suffering from the effect of aspartame is memory loss.

It has been shown that ingesting aspartame, especially along with carbohydrates, can lead to excess levels of phenylalanine in the brain.

Excessive levels of phenylalanine in the brain can cause the levels of serotonin in the brain to decrease, leading to emotional disorders such as depression.

Excessive buildup of phenylalanine in the brain can cause schizophrenia or make one more susceptible to seizures.

Methanol/wood alcohol is a deadly poison that makes up 10% of aspartame.

One account of a case of extremely high phenylalanine levels caused by aspartame was recently published the "Wednesday Journal" in an article titled "An Aspartame Nightmare." John Cook began drinking six to eight diet drinks every day. His symptoms started out as memory loss and frequent headaches. He began to crave more aspartame-sweetened drinks. His condition deteriorated so much that he experienced wide mood swings and violent rages. Even though he did not suffer from PKU, a blood test revealed a phenylalanine level of 80 mg/dl. He also showed abnormal brain function and brain damage. After he kicked his aspartame habit, his symptoms improved dramatically.

As Blaylock points out in his book, early studies measuring phenylalanine buildup in the brain were flawed. Investigators who measured specific brain regions and not the average throughout the brain notice significant rises in phenylalanine levels. Specifically the hypothalamus, medulla oblongata, and corpus striatum areas of the brain had the largest increases in phenylalanine. Blaylock goes on to point out that excessive buildup of phenylalanine in the brain can cause schizophrenia or make one more susceptible to seizures.

Therefore, long-term, excessive use of aspartame may provide a boost to sales of serotonin re-uptake inhibitors such as Prozac and drugs to control schizophrenia and seizures.

3. Methanol (aka wood alcohol/poison) (10 percent of aspartame)

Methanol/wood alcohol is a deadly poison. Some people may remember methanol as the poison that has caused some "skid row" alcoholics to end up blind or dead. Methanol is gradually released in the small intestine when the methyl group of aspartame encounter the enzyme chymotrypsin.

The absorption of methanol into the body is sped up considerably when free methanol is ingested. Free methanol is created from aspartame when it is heated to above 86 Fahrenheit (30 Centigrade). This would occur when an aspartame-containing product is improperly stored or when it is heated (e.g., as part of a "food" product such as Jello).

Methanol breaks down into formic acid and formaldehyde in the body. Formaldehyde is a deadly neurotoxin. An EPA assessment of methanol states that methanol "is considered a cumulative poison due to the low rate of excretion once it is absorbed. In the body, methanol is oxidized to formaldehyde and formic acid; both of these metabolites are toxic." They recommend a limit of consumption of 7.8 mg/day. A one-liter (approx. 1 quart) aspartame-sweetened beverage contains about 56 mg of methanol. Heavy users of aspartame-containing products consume as much as 250 mg of methanol daily or 32 times the EPA limit.

Symptoms from methanol poisoning include headaches, ear buzzing, dizziness, nausea, gastrointestinal disturbances, weakness, vertigo, chills, memory lapses, numbness and shooting pains in the extremities, behavioral disturbances, and neuritis. The most well known problems from methanol poisoning are vision problems including misty vision, progressive contraction of visual fields, blurring of vision, and obscuration of vision, retinal damage, and blindness.

Formaldehyde is a known carcinogen, causes retinal damage, interferes with DNA replication and causes birth defects.

Due to the lack of a couple of key enzymes, humans are many times more sensitive to the toxic effects of methanol than animals. Therefore, tests of aspartame or methanol on animals do not accurately reflect the danger for humans. As pointed out by Dr. Woodrow C. Monte, director of the food science and nutrition laboratory at Arizona State University, "There are no human or mammalian studies to evaluate the possible mutagenic, teratogenic or carcinogenic effects of chronic administration of methyl alcohol."

He was so concerned about the unresolved safety issues that he filed suit with the FDA requesting a hearing to address these issues. He asked the FDA to "slow down on this soft drink issue long enough to answer some of the important questions. It's not fair that you are leaving the full burden of proof on the few of us who are concerned and have such limited resources.

You must remember that you are the American public's last defense. Once you allow usage (of aspartame) there is literally nothing that can be done to reverse the course. Aspartame will then join saccharin, the sulfating agents, and how many other questionable compounds enjoined to insult the human constitution with governmental approval." Shortly thereafter, the Commissioner of the FDA, Arthur Hull Hayes, Jr., approved the use of aspartame in carbonated beverages, he then left for a position with G.D. Searle's public relations firm.

It has been pointed out that some fruit juices and alcoholic beverages contain small amounts of methanol. It is important to remember, however, that methanol never appears alone. In every case, ethanol is present, usually in much higher amounts. Ethanol is an

Formaldehyde is a known carcinogen, causes retinal damage, interferes with DNA replication and causes birth defects.

Once you allow usage (of aspartame) there is literally nothing that can be done to reverse the course.

143

antidote for methanol toxicity in humans. The troops of Desert Storm were "treated" to large amounts of aspartame-sweetened beverages, which had been heated to over 86 degrees F in the Saudi Arabian sun. Many of them returned home with numerous disorders similar to what has been seen in persons who have been chemically poisoned by formaldehyde. The free methanol in the beverages may have been a contributing factor in these illnesses. Other breakdown products of aspartame such as DKP (discussed below) may also have been a factor.

In a 1993 act that can only be described as "unconscionable," the FDA approved aspartame as an ingredient in numerous food items that would always be heated to above 86 degree F (30 degree C).

Diketopiperazine (DKP)

DKP is a byproduct of aspartame metabolism. DKP has been implicated in the occurrence of brain tumors. Olney noticed that DKP, when nitrosated in the gut, produced a compound that was similar to N-nitrosourea, a powerful brain tumor causing chemical. Some authors have said that DKP is produced after aspartame ingestion. I am not sure if that is correct. It is definitely true that DKP is formed in liquid aspartame-containing products during prolonged storage.

G.D. Searle conducted animal experiments on the safety of DKP. The FDA found numerous experimental errors occurred, including "clerical errors, mixed-up animals, animals not getting drugs they were supposed to get, pathological specimens lost because of improper handling," and many other errors. These sloppy laboratory procedures may explain why both the test and control animals had sixteen times more brain tumors than would be expected in experiments of this length.

In an ironic twist, shortly after these experimental errors were discovered, the FDA used guidelines recommended by G.D. Searle to develop the industry-wide FDA standards for good laboratory practices.

DKP has also been implicated as a cause of uterine polyps and changes in blood cholesterol by FDA Toxicologist Dr. Jacqueline Verrett in her testimony before the U.S. Senate.

Aspartame Warning

The multi-billion dollar aspartame industry would like you believe that "aspartame kills" is an "urban legend" and that you'd have to drink 100 cans of diet soda a day to be harmed by aspartame. This is just simply not true. Their main claim is that the 3 components of aspartame are found in many natural foods and are therefore safe. This is kind of like saying carbon monoxide is safe because all it contains is carbon & oxygen, the same components of carbon dioxide. Methanol (wood alcohol), which makes up 10% of aspartame and is highly toxic (adult minimum lethal dose is 2 teaspoons), is also found in some fruits & vegetables like tomatoes.

However, methanol is never found in natural foods without **ethanol** and pectin, its "antidotes" if you will (detailed facts below). Ethanol and pectin prevent methanol from being metabolized into **formaldehyde** (embalming fluid) and formic acid (same chemical as fire ant venom), both deadly toxins. An ethanol drip is even the standard emergency room treatment for methanol poisoning. Aspartame contains no ethanol or pectin, therefore the methanol is converted to formaldehyde and formic acid. Phenylalanine and aspartic acid, the other 2 components of aspartame, are amino acids found in natural foods but always as part of long chains of many different amino acids to form complex protein molecules that take humans 12 hours to gradually break down and assimilate. When consumed by themselves these 2 amino acids require no digestion and quickly enter the brain and central nervous system at abnormally high levels, over stimulating brain cells to death and causing many other health problems.

"Pro" aspartame people point to industry sponsored short term tests, ignoring independent tests. They point to "reliable" health sites, organizations, foundations etc. that are sponsored, funded and fed "facts" by companies that profit from aspartame. And of course, the FDA approved it so "it must be safe", neglecting to mention that the **FDA denied aspartame approval** for over 8 years until the newly appointed FDA commissioner Arthur Hull Hayes **overruled** the final scientific review panel, approved aspartame, and then went to work for G.D. Searle's (initial owner of aspartame) public relations firm at $1,000 a day. Hayes has refused all interviews to discuss his actions. The FDA also urged Congress to prosecute G.D. Searle for "specific false statements or concealed facts" stemming from Searle's testing of aspartame. However, the 2 government lawyers assigned to the case decided against prosecuting G.D. Searle and then joined G.D. Searle's law firm! Even the National Soft Drink Assn. filed a strong protest letter in 1983 against the approval of aspartame for use in beverages, saying "aspartame is inherently, markedly and uniquely unstable in aqueous media." Also, the FDA still allows hydrogenated oils to be used, does that make them safe?

Methanol is never found in natural foods without ethanol & pectin, its "antidotes" if you will Ethanol & pectin prevent methanol from being metabolized into formaldehyde (embalming fluid) and formic acid (same chemical as fire ant venom), both deadly toxins.

Even the National Soft Drink Assn. filed a strong protest letter in 1983 against the approval of aspartame for use in beverages, saying "aspartame is inherently, markedly and uniquely unstable in aqueous media."

145

Is There a Natural Alternative to Sugar?

Yes — Stevia is a natural sugar alternative.

Stevia is a natural, sweet-tasting, non-toxic plant that has no calories, lowers blood pressure, and inhibits fat absorption. It is diabetic-safe as it does not adversely affect blood sugar. It is heat stable to 200 degrees Celsius (392 degrees Fahrenheit) so is safe for use in cooking and can be added to hot drinks. It is said to be 10-40 times sweeter than sugar and can be bought in both powder and liquid form.

Japan has been using stevia instead of sugar to sweeten many food products, such as ice cream, bread, candies, pickles, soft drinks and chewing gum, since the mid 1970s. By the late 1980s, stevia represented approximately 41 percent of the market share of potently sweet products consumed in Japan.

Other countries using Stevia today include Thailand, China, South Korea, Paraguay, and Brazil.

In fact, Stevia has been used around the world for at least 1500 years with no reported side-effects, yet it has not been approved as a food additive in the US because "We don't have enough data to conclude that the use (in food) would be safe" (quoted from an agency position paper).

(Aspartame, on the other hand, is a constant source of complaint. A former FDA investigator admits that approximately 75 percent of all the 'adverse reaction' complaints the FDA receives are related to aspartame!)

There will be no race to test Stevia for approval while there is big money to be made from chemical substances such as aspartame because being a natural substance Stevia can't be patented by the huge pharmaceutical corporations.

Though not yet approved in the US as a food additive, Stevia can be sold, and consumed, as a 'dietary supplement.' In what way the FDA can justify how a natural food substance is safe as a supplement but unsafe as an additive is puzzling.

> Stevia is a natural, sweet-tasting, non-toxic plant that has no calories, lowers blood pressure and inhibits fat absorption.

> Though not yet approved in the US as a food additive, Stevia can be sold, and consumed, as a 'dietary supplement.'

147

Stevia in the UK?

In the UK it is not possible to buy stevia from shops or other suppliers. The EU have totally banned sales and use of stevia for any purpose. So, in the EU the choice seems to be between the empty calories of sugar and the chemical toxins of aspartame.

Luckily, you can order stevia over the internet from several companies.

Life is Sweet

If you are looking for a healthy (and readily available) alternative to refined sugar and chemical sweeteners, one of the best is blackstrap molasses. This contains calcium, iron, and B vitamins, and it has about a quarter of the calories of refined sugar.

But the best source of sweetness must come from fruit. There are so many varieties of sweet fruits — enough to satisfy the sweetest tooth. With fruits and vegetables making up about 80% of your diet (in an ideal world) you should get all the sweetness you need naturally with no additives.

The EU have totally banned sales and use of stevia for any purpose.

The best source of sweetness must come from fruit.

SECTION THREE:

The Healing Power of Alkaline Water

The Healing Power of Alkaline Water

Huge impurities that are often found in regular tap water

Alkaline water is simply water that has been processed to remove the ions that create acidity inside the body. While removing the acidic ions, impurities are also removed, creating a water that increases alkalinity inside the body and is completely pure and healthier for your system. **If you have heard about the huge impurities that are often found in regular tap water, you will see why so many professionals are now backing up the concept of alkaline water.** Those who drink this type of water report that it tastes so much better than ordinary tap water and even bottled water thanks to the increased purity. It is also complimentary to an anti-acidity diet for anyone trying to produce the healthiest internal environment for their overall health.

In order to create this type of pure water for your own consumption, you need an ionizing purification system. Ionized water is simply passed through a water ionizer to take out impurities and acidic ions before delivering it to your glass. There is some expense with installing this type of purification system, but the added health benefits are far worth the investment!

Ion purifiers are still the preferred method since they deliver purer water and are more efficient at creating internal alkalinity.

Some other methods of creating alkaline water which are not nearly as effective include mineral drops that will turn the water more in the direction of alkalinity and special filters which the water can pass through to remove the ions. Magnetic fields have also proven to work to some extent, but the ion purifiers are still the preferred method since they deliver purer water and are more efficient at creating internal alkalinity.

Could alkaline water really be the missing link to a long, healthy life full of energy and a greater sense of well being? Many professionals and doctors say "YES!" They believe it is one critical link to a healthy lifestyle since it removes some of the impurities that are commonly found inside the human body and it helps establish a more natural condition inside the body.

Alkaline water can be created using a water ionizer.

A water ionizer creates a kind of water that is very beneficial to the human body. This is especially true for someone that follows a typical western diet. As most of us are aware, a western diet includes junk food, fast food, soda, processed and packaged foods, and pretty much anything that is not made the way Mother Nature intended. In other words, it is a very acidic diet. These excess acids pool in our bodies creating all kinds of havoc. It ranges from low energy and obesity to cancer.

Water ionizers have the ability to transform regular tap water into ionized alkaline water.

As the water passes through the water ionizer and is filtered, an electric charge is applied to the water by electrodes. This electric charge ionizes and changes the water molecules structurally and electrically, and it endows them with a myriad of health benefits.

My Own Experience

I will never forget the first time I tasted alkaline water. Unless you have tried it for yourself my description would hardly do it justice. The very first thing I noticed was how easy and smooth it was to drink. It almost has a velvet kind of consistency compared to the harshness of normal tap water. I did some further investigating and found out that 'ionization' which is the process for making alkaline water breaks clusters of water molecules into smaller micro-clusters. This greatly reduces the size of the clusters from the 11-16 molecules in standard water to just 5-6 molecules in ionized water. **Smaller clusters pass through cell walls more easily and hydrate the cells more quickly.** This explained why it went down so much easier than normal drinking water.

It wasn't very long before I started to notice significant differences in my health and energy levels.

What's interesting is that due to the size, micro-clusters of ionized water molecules are expelled from the cells more efficiently, carrying damaging toxins out of the cells and flushing them out of the system.

A higher pH level in the body also reduces the need for fat and cholesterol to protect the body from damaging acids.

One of the leading causes of obesity is due to the body being forced to produce an unhealthy amount of fat cells just to stop the acidity from burning holes inside of you.

I also started to notice that cooking with alkaline water improved the taste of foods and I found that it also enhanced the taste of various herbal teas. Cooking with normal water only adds more acidity to your diet and not to mentioned all of the other unfiltered microbes that you might be digesting. By the way, boiling the water does not kill all bacteria nor does it get rid of fluoride.

Dr. Robert Young, author of The pH Miracle, is the world's leading expert when it comes to the acid/alkaline balance in our diet. **He was believed to be the first to medically document a Type 1 Diabetes reversal.** He has also helped patients reverse many forms of cancer including aggressive cancers and he did it without the use of chemo, surgery, or drugs.

But how can that be?

We've been told that cancer is a horrible disease that can happen to any of us. But Dr. Young states that **cancer is really nothing more than excess acids built up in your tissues.**

So how does he reverse these diseases?

He does this by teaching people to change their dietary habits which means increasing the amount of raw green vegetables and he teaches them to start drinking a lot of alkaline ionized water.

Alkaline water is very different from what you will find in your tap or in a bottle for three very specific reasons.

The first is the pH.

A water ionizer will allow you to increase the pH to your desired amount. Water has a pH of 7 and is considered neutral on the pH scale. You can increase the pH to 8 or 9 giving you 10 times to 100 times the alkalinity of regular water. This will neutralize those acids in your tissues.

The second benefit is the antioxidant power.

This can only come from using a water ionizer. It may come as a surprise to you, but bottled water and tap water are oxidizing to the body.

The third benefit is smaller water clusters.

Did you ever drink water and felt like you were still thirsty? This is because of the large water clusters. The smaller water clusters are easily

153

absorbed into your tissues creating a "wetter" water. Your thirst is quenched because your tissues are getting the benefit of a better water.

The fourth benefit is cost.

How much do you spend each year on bottled water? A water ionizer can cost less than bottled water and you are providing your family with healthier water.

What kind of price can you put on your family's health?

The alkaline water benefits can be made possible when you see just how much better the water actually is.

How Water Ionizers Work

The newest phenomenon in the society of physical condition has become the most recent way to strengthen your overall well-being at the push of a button. By using a system called electrolysis, alkaline water machines supposedly separate the positively and negatively charged molecules in the water. Depending on the setting, this separation of molecules will deliver either alkaline or acidic water. **The greater pH of the water has been said to reduce the effects of toxins in the body and raise the immune system.** Many who perform alternative medicine believe that many illnesses and other bodily sicknesses can be relieved simply by raising the alkalinity of the body. Since cancer cells can't exist in an alkaline environment, is said to be a excellent way to stop cancer and other degenerative illnesses including cancer, diabetes, and arthritis.

Because minerals need to be dissolved in the water in order to ionize it, authorities of alternative medicine also believe in the ability of to fortify bone structures and prevent osteoporosis. **The human body immediately strives to maintain a certain amount of alkalinity. If an individual isn't receiving enough minerals in their water, the body will balance out by drawing valuable minerals such as calcium and magnesium from bones.**

Another benefit is that because it is built of smaller clusters of molecules, it is much more quickly absorbed into cells and the bloodstream. This not only benefits in the eradicating of toxins, but better overall hydration. **Individuals who have begun drinking alkaline water report almost instantaneous boosts in energy and enlarged vitality**.

Many who perform alternative medicine believe that many illnesses and other bodily sicknesses can be relieved simply by raising the alkalinity of the body.

Since cancer cells can't exist in an alkaline environment, is said to be a excellent way to stop cancer and other degenerative illnesses including cancer, diabetes, and arthritis.

Since water is one of the main components of living organisms, it's no surprise that keeping properly hydrated is one of the best strategies to boost overall health. **Alkaline water is one of the most desired forms of alternative medicine on the market.** Experts believe that the eradicating of toxins from the body and faster absorption of water into the cells is critical to preserving optimum health and enhancing the immune system.

According to Dr. Hidemitsu Hayashi, M.D., director of the Water Institute of Japan, it's the smaller sized molecule clusters and heightened pH that gives alkaline water its fitness positive aspects. **He feels that ionized water is greater because it is the most convenient way to maximize oxygen levels in the bloodstream and grants the water an easier time with absorbing into cells.** Hidemitsu thinks that getting rid of acidic substances in our body and keeping properly hydrated is the simplest way to prevent disease and encourage an overall better status of health.

The Importance pH Balance

pH levels can be affected by diet as well as the pollution in the atmosphere. Eating foods that have a high-alkaline value can also restore alkaline levels, but nothing works as fast as alkaline water. Maintaining pH balance is hard in today's age of sodas and fast food.

Alkaline water is not at all acidic, but it has more alkalinity than normal water. Normal water is supposed to have a pH level of 7, but alkaline water has a pH level of 8 or more. This water is not neutral on the pH levels. It has a more alkalinity than normal water. It is usually devoid of any acid. **It works like antacid.** It neutralizes acid in chemical solutions. This water is also known as ionized water.

The main use of alkaline water is drinking it as normal water. **Ionized water or alkaline water is known to balance the pH level in the human body, thus benefiting the body in the process.** Alkaline water is found in bottles 'in the market'. Ionized water is costly, but there is an alternate way to get ionized water. The problem is that one has to spend a small fortune to get a water ionizer. **Water ionizers are fitted to any normal tap.** Fitting a water ionizer is a good choice, as it can provide ionized water for the whole family and it supplies the water 24/7.

Water ionizers can be extremely expensive. Some ionizers cost more than one thousand dollars. It is hard for most people to spend that much at once, but spending on bottled ionized water may be much more expensive in

Alkaline water is one of the most desired forms of alternative medicine on the market.

Alkaline water is usually devoid of any acid.

the long run.

Let us now discuss the benefits of ionized water. **The cells in your body are alkaline based.** This means it needs alkaline to maintain proper functionality, but when the cells work it releases metabolic waste. This waste is acidic in nature. The cells use this waste as an energy source, but if the produced waste isn't put to use it builds up in the body.

As this waste is acidic in nature, it increases the acid level in the body. This in turn, affects the pH balance in the body. If acids soar, the pH balance in the body has to suffer. The body uses nutrients of other organs to maintain the alkaline level of the cells. This weakens the other organs of the body thus weakening the body. It is important to keep a good pH balance in the body. <u>It is the key to good health</u>. Some scientist thinks that pH levels are the first defense against diseases. **The body has its own complex system of cleaning. It overloads when the acid levels rises.**

Some diseases are directly related to acid levels.

Because of the fact that some diseases are directly related to acid levels — keeping your pH balance is very important. Having an ideal pH balance means having a healthy body and alkaline water helps to get the acid level down and maintain a proper alkaline level.

An alkaline water ionizer will take regular tap water and produce energized water or alkaline ionized water which is essentially what we are made of and what we need to live.

The average person can live without food from 4 to 6 weeks. Living without water will depend on how much excursion you put out (how much sweat) and the current temperature of the environment you are in. Without water at a temperature of 120 F/48.9 C you could survive for 2 days. At 50 F / 10.0 C, 60 F / 15.6 C or 70 F / 21.1 C you would survive for 10 days. Needless to say we cannot live without water.

Now the water that most people consume on a daily basis is not that healthy. You might be saying to yourself right now that "I don't drink tap water, I drink bottled so I'm safe".

Unfortunately this is not the case.

First I'd like you to read this quote regarding plastic bottles used for bottled water.

"But no one should think that bottled water is better regulated, better protected or safer than tap," said Eric Goldstein, co-director of the urban program at the Natural Resources Defense Council (NRDC), a nonprofit organization devoted to protecting health and the environment. Most people are surprised to learn that they're drinking glorified tap water, but bottlers aren't required to list the source on the label

Most bottled water comes in polyethylene terephthalate bottles, indicated by a number 1, PET, or PETE on the bottle's bottom. The bottles are generally safe, says Ken Smith, PhD, immediate past chair of the American Chemical Society's division of environmental chemistry. **But scientists say when stored in hot or warm temperatures, the plastic may leak chemicals into the water.**

We already knew that tap water isn't the healthiest water to drink, now we understand that drinking bottled water really isn't that much better. And don't get me started on the incredible amount of waste created with all of these plastic bottles.

The main point of this article is to inform you that the best possible water you can drink is alkaline ionized water.

Alkaline water is water that is above the neutral pH level which is considered to be 7.0 pH. When the pH of the body gets out of balance (too acidic), we may experience low energy, fatigue, excess weight, poor digestion, aches and pains, and even more serious disorders. **Our bodies consist of over 70% water.** The most optimum pH level to be at is a slightly alkaline range of about 7.3 pH.

The best way to maintain these healthy pH levels and keep your body at its peak operating performance is by drinking water after it has gone through a alkaline water ionizer.

According to my research I found that alkaline water was able to neutralize the acidity build up in the body caused mainly by stress, modern diet, pollution in the air and even by certain brands of bottled water. The pH level of our blood fluctuates between 7.35 — 7.45 which on a pH scale is slightly alkaline. **If the blood was to deviate even slightly from this figure**

But scientists say that bottled water is stored in hot or warm temperatures, the plastic may leak chemicals into the water.

The pH level of our blood fluctuates between 7.35 — 7.45 which on a pH scale is slightly alkaline. If the blood was to deviate even slightly from this figure we could potentially die.

we could potentially die.

Acidity build-up in the body also creates the appropriate environment for many types of disease to flourish and expand. Scientists have found that cancer cells and tumors feed on acidity and are able to proliferate in an acidic environment. **By drinking alkaline water on a daily basis you are neutralizing the acidity and free radicals in your body that we are bombarded with on a regular basis.** This whole concept made a lot of sense to me and I decided to venture out and purchase myself a good quality alkaline ionizer. There seem to be a lot of choices on the market but abiding by the rules of 'you get what you pay for' I decided to spend that little bit extra and get myself a reputable and good quality unit.

You Must Drink The Very Best Water

Water is the basic necessity for any living body on this planet. Without which the process of surviving would be a difficult task. And as the population is increasing, so is the consumption. All of us must have read articles in newspapers or health magazines regarding the recommended daily intake of water to help our body function smoothly and effectively: Doctors say that a human body must consume at least 8 glasses of water a day. But the question here is: **If intake of water is so important, then should we not make sure that every sip of water that we gulp down must be pure and harmless?**

Water comprises approximately 70% of an adult human body and, scientifically, our bodies can afford to lose only 2% of its water content so we need to keep our bodies well hydrated to maintain this water percentage.

Dehydration in the body can, at the least, cause problems like...

- Excessive thirst
- Fatigue
- Dry mouth
- Dizziness
- Low blood pressure
- Little or no urination
- Headache
- Nausea

> By drinking alkaline water on a daily basis you are neutralizing the acidity and free radicals in your body that we are bombarded with on a regular basis.

> If intake of water is so important, then should we not make sure that every sip of water that we gulp down must be pure and harmless?

158

- Light-headedness

Now that we have proved the importance of intake of pure water, we must further focus on the ways by which we can provide ourselves with it. This brings up the topic of the use and importance of ALKALINE WATER. Medical studies have proved that alkaline water has the most powerful anti-oxidant properties, better than vitamins A, C, D, beta carotene, and selenium which improves our body defense system against diseases.

HOW DO WE PRODUCE ALKALINE WATER?

The three main methods to obtain alkaline water are...

- Using a water ionizer

- Using a distiller

- Adding alkaline ingredients to water

An IONIZER is more than just a water filter, it is a system which changes structure of water into an ionized state. This ionized water in turn is used for several benefits by its users.

The DISTILLER is used to convert normal water into distilled water. Distilled water is the water which is first turned into steam and then condensed back to water. This process kills all impurities in water and makes the water pH slightly alkaline. This is one of the best way of getting alkaline water.

Adding alkaline ingredients to water:

- Adding lemon water — lemon water is very alkaline and is great in detoxifying liver and kidney. Also (or lime) water has always helped in distressing ourselves in the times of great fatigue.

- pH drops — these drops add instant alkalinity to water and gives incredible boost to the one drinking it.

BENEFITS OF MAKING THE WATER ALKALINE:

Here is a list of benefits you would achieve if you use alkaline water for drinking, cooking your daily food, or in your beverages: It would give increased clarity of mind and understanding. Due to extra oxygen in the ionized alkaline water which helps the brain function more efficiently.

An IONIZER is more than just a water filter, it is a system which changes structure of water into an ionized state.

> Helps to keep your body pH levels balanced saving you from unnecessary fatigue and laziness.

> Helps in losing weight

> Better absorption of nutrients from the food we eat

> Helps reduce wrinkles and age spots

Drinking hefty amounts of water daily is good for your health and aids your weight loss efforts, no one argues with this fact. **But many still do not know that they can get the added benefits of alkaline water when they make it a choice for their daily dose of water.** Being the healthiest type of drinking water, it contributes greatly to a cleaner, more energized body in the form of crystal clear freshness. You get the ionized advantage in your water, the same way it has been performed for ages in those blue glacial streams and icebergs.

Why not just tap and bottled water? Well, tap and bottled water are still the most frequently consumed by people. **The sources of tap water surely pose harmful bacteria and elements due to uncertain treatments, and as for bottled water, this expensive option also means taking in too much acid and toxins leached from the bottles used.** On the other hand, cleaner water and a healthier drinking lifestyle are some of the major benefits of alkaline water.

You ask, what is it and how is it beneficial to people? It is water that goes through an ionization process and renders the drink filled with minerals helpful to your body's functions as it hydrates your cells sufficiently.

Drinking alkaline water alone ups your body's hydration level to six times more than just tap and bottled water. With this, you will experience an increase in your body's energy as it rehydrates all systems that you need to keep you active.

Because alkaline water has negative oxidation reduction potential (ORP), it increases the level of oxygen in your body and neutralizes harmful free radicals. With this process, you get the additional benefit of alkaline water as a natural antioxidant.

Another, among the numerous benefits, is that **it reduces symptoms of aging and prevents sickness and chronic diseases from setting in.** This is

Being the healthiest type of drinking water, it contributes greatly to a cleaner, more energized body in the form of crystal clear freshness.

Ionized is water that goes through an ionization process, and renders the drink filled with minerals helpful to your body's functions as it hydrates your cells sufficiently.

Another among the numerous benefits is that it reduces symptoms of aging and prevents sickness and chronic diseases from setting in.

because water with a higher pH has components of a natural antacid and, being so, it neutralizes the acidity in your body and helps fight off illnesses.

Distilled water and de-ionized water does not have the benefits of alkaline water. Where **conventional water from the local water system is unsafe as they carry potential harm from seepages,** alkaline water that has gone through an ionizer means you're drinking that pure, fresh liquid free of bacteria and harmful chemicals. Where bottled waters are not fully distilled and de-ionized, alkaline water from your home ionizer is guaranteed a safer choice. Where other packaged waters lose their negative charge inside the bottles, water flowing from your ionizer is definitely a healthy drink.

Alkaline water is gaining in recognition and popularity among alternative health professionals and consumers alike. It is slowly becoming accepted that an alkalizing diet may have a positive impact on health and vitality. Just as you need to look after the pH level of your pool, your body also has a pH level that needs to be kept in balance too.

The alkalinity of water is measured by what is called the pH level which stands for 'potential of hydrogen.' The pH scale ranges from 0 on the acidic end, to 14 on the alkaline end with 7 being neutral. So waters with a pH reading below 7 is acidic and those above 7 are alkaline. Many people wrongly assume all drinking water is neutral. The fact is, distilled water is neutral while most of the drinking water available to us is acidic. Alkaline water is also considered to be water with more oxygen.

The Three Benefits of Alkaline Water:

1. **Restores The pH Balance of The Body**

   • Alkaline water can neutralize the acidity of the body caused by stress, modern diet, air pollution, and many bottled waters.

   • A higher pH in the body reduces the need for fat and cholesterol to protect the body from damaging acids.

   • Improves body function by cleaning your cells from the inside out.

2. **Detoxifies Cells More Efficiently Than Standard Drinking Water.**

   • The negative charge of ionized alkaline water will attract the positive

> Alkaline water that has gone through an ionizer means you're drinking that pure, fresh liquid free of bacteria and harmful chemicals.

> The alkalinity of water is measured by what is called the pH level which stands for 'potential of hydrogen.'

161

ions of acids and neutralize them within the body.

- Due to their smaller size, micro-clusters of ionized water molecules are expelled from the cells more efficiently carrying damaging toxins (which also causes weight gain in individuals) out of the cells and flushing them out of the system.

3. Slows Aging and Helps With Weight Loss.

- It is also true that food cravings are often the body's cry for water. You might already have more of a thirst than you even realize — and if you are going to quench it, make sure your water is alkaline!

- It stops free radicals from forming, flushes toxins from cells, and prevents toxins from accumulating, provides essential minerals, promotes normal blood flow, and maintains normal blood pH. Alkaline water also is said to be better at hydrating the body because it penetrates cells more effectively.

Is Alkaline Water The Cure For Diabetes?

As you no doubt know, if you suffer from Diabetes, there are two main categories of Diabetes: Type 1 diabetes, also called Insulin-Dependent Diabetes, usually occurs in young people and is the second most common chronic disease in children (after asthma). In this condition the pancreas produces a minimal amount of insulin and daily injections are needed to make up the deficit. Type 2 diabetes, also called Adult-Onset Diabetes, has historically occurred almost exclusively in adults and is generally triggered by dietary habits which continuously spike the blood sugar and finally exhaust the pancreas.

But here is the shocking reality of the recent outcome of our children's lifestyle and dietary habits: Children of ages of 15 to 19 years are now the fastest growing group to contract this disease.

Type 2 diabetes now accounts for ninety percent of all diabetes cases and is the fastest-growing disease in North America... but it doesn't need to be like this!

And another shocking reality: Type 2 is not only preventable it has been shown to be completely reversible in many, many cases using completely natural means without drugs.

That's right... alkaline ionized water, the right diet, exercise, and a healthy balanced lifestyle can generate remarkable reversals in this condition in a very short time.

Many scientists are now of the opinion that not only is Type 2 Diabetes controllable but is reversible without drugs. **Inadequate hydration and an acid pH balance in the body, coupled with free radical damage, are now considered major culprits in the growth of diabetes.**

Clinical trials of diabetic patients were run in a Korean hospital and reported by MBC TV in a program called the "Truth about Water of Life." The patients were divided into two groups: one group continued with their usual insulin protocol while the second group ceased their insulin injections and instead drank only ionized alkaline water.

Dr. Won H. Kim, whose background includes a doctorate from Oxford University in biochemistry, is a Professor at the Medical School at Yonsei University, Seoul, South Korea. In his book "Water of Life" he reports as follows on the above trials:

"In less than one month the blood sugar level of the group drinking alkaline water had amazingly decreased in contrast to that of the insulin-injection group. Daily fluctuations in blood sugar continued to occur in the case of the insulin group, while those drinking the alkaline water maintained remarkably stable levels."

This result is quite extraordinary!

Ordinary tap water can be run through an alkaline water ionizer and produce both short-term and long-term relief for diabetes sufferers. And **this ionized water is rich in negative ions which act as a powerful anti-oxidant to neutralize the hordes of free radicals in our bodies.**

When a molecule loses an electron, it is called a Free Radical.

Oxygen is about the 4th most reactive of all of the elements. That's why iron rusts and apples go brown so readily.

The most violent of the free radicals in our bodies are created from Oxygen molecules.

Many scientists are now of the opinion that not only is Type II Diabetes controllable but is reversible without drugs.

Ordinary tap water can be run through an alkaline water ionizer and produce both short term and long term relief for diabetes sufferers.

Here's what happens:

All elements except Hydrogen and Helium want to have 8 electrons in their outer levels. Only the inert elements like Neon and Argon have 8 naturally. Oxygen has 6 and is always looking to find another 2 electrons to make it complete. Without the 8 electrons it is highly reactive.

Hydrogen has one electron in its outer level so two hydrogens combine with one oxygen to make water. **Oxygen borrows the two electrons from the hydrogen to make itself complete.**

In the atmosphere oxygen exists as a molecule that contains two atoms — the formula is O2. A good model is to think of O2 as two atoms side by side, each having four electrons on the outer edges and sharing 2 electrons from each atom in the middle, so each atom feels it has eight — four on the outside and four in the middle..

When a molecule loses an electron it is called a Free Radical.

In the metabolism of food or just in breathing, especially when doing cardio, the Oxygen molecule loses an electron during the reaction so it no longer feels complete and is continually looking for another electron to steal. It happens with other molecules like nitrogen too, but oxygen is involved in most of the metabolism reactions and is by far the most aggressive. **Because Oxygen is so reactive when it steals the electron from a tissue or a molecule inside the cell walls it causes damage.** At the cellular lever an oxygen free radical is so aggressive it actually burns holes in the cell walls and causes eventual mutations of the DNA as it steals electrons from there.

This is how cancer is born.

An "Anti-oxidant" is something that neutralizes the aggressive nature of the free radical by supplying it with the electrons it needs or with a negative ion to fill the gap. Vitamin C and Vitamin E, etc., do this, but **highly Ionized Alkaline water has a huge supply of free electrons and negatively charges "OH" ions just looking for something like a Free Radical to neutralize themselves.**

Supply enough free electrons and the Oxygen free radicals calm down for awhile.

The number of free positive or negative charges in a fluid are

measured by ORP — Oxidation/Reduction Potential. Reduction is simply the opposite of the Oxidation process. A positive reading — meaning lots of free positive charges is bad. A negative reading — meaning lots of free negative charges or electrons is good.

Ionized Alkaline water has 8 times as much ORP as Vitamin C and is the best Anti-oxidant we have heard of.

This is why the ORP is even more critical than the alkalinity.

Water is not really H_2O — it is H and OH. When we split the water into the acid and alkaline streams using ionization we actually drag the H-OH molecule apart. We send an excess of Hydrogen ions (positive charges) down the acid pipe and an equal excess of OH ions (negative charges) down the alkaline pipe. We supply both Alkalinity and an excess of Free Electrons from the alkaline pipe that are not matched by an equal number of positive charges.

Most alkaline solutions have an equal number of positive and negative charges making them electrically neutral but Ionized Alkaline water is in effect electrically negatively charged. This is why ionization of water works so well.

Here are 3 more health benefits provided by ionized alkaline water:

1) Alkaline Water is More Hydrating Than Tap Water

How is it possible that this new water could be more hydrating than regular water? Is not water just water? During the ionization process, the shape of the water molecules is slightly changed. The molecules become smaller and the water molecule clusters obtain a hexagonal configuration. This new more compact water molecule can now more easily penetrate the tissues of the body. This results in more overall hydration as well as greater detoxification of the tissues. Hydration is increased six-fold with alkaline water.

2) Hypertension is Decreased by Ionized Alkaline Water

About one in three adults in the US suffer from high blood pressure or hypertension. There are many contributing factors that may lead to the condition. One of the factors related to high blood pressure is that less

Ionized Alkaline water has 8 times as much ORP as Vitamin C and is the best Anti-oxidant we have heard of.

Most alkaline solutions have an equal number of positive and negative charges making them electrically neutral but Ionized Alkaline water is in effect electrically negatively charged.

oxygen is absorbed by the body. There is a connection to the pH level in your body. Notice when you take a couple of deep breaths before you check your blood pressure, the results are always better than when the blood pressure is taken without the breaths. More oxygen in your body makes your body pH slightly more basic or alkaline, lowering your blood pressure. Ionized alkaline water on a daily basis can aid in keeping your blood pressure low by keeping your system alkaline.

3) Alkaline Water Helps to Maintain an Ideal Body Weight

Obesity in the United States is a problem of epidemic proportions. This condition now even affects children in the US, and morbid obesity is on the rise. There are many reported reasons and theories as to why that is. Some reasons may be cultural eating habits, lack of exercise, over consumption of sugar, soft drinks, alcohol, and red meat. It is amazing the quantities of soda drinks we consume in the US. We are also not generally accustomed to eating enough vegetables in this country.

Consuming high amounts of carbonated water, alcohol, and sugar can render any human body toxic and acidic. The body reacts to toxins and acidity by surrounding the organs with more fat. By consuming ionized alkaline water on a daily basis in conjunction with a high alkaline low sugar diet, you can naturally maintain a healthy body weight.

Nature has provided "miracle waters" in only five places in the world, Japan being one of them. In every one of these places, the native people enjoy long and healthy lives. The secret is in the water. These waters are clean, alkaline, micro-clustered, anti-oxidant waters. The Japanese drink this alkaline water.

Is it possible that the health we desire is as simple as changing the water we drink?

I think so. **The American diet consists primarily of acid forming foods.** Our daily lives are often so stress-related with stress causing a high production of adrenaline which is a naturally acidic compound. Our environment has become increasingly toxic, exposing us daily to toxic chemicals we breathe and absorb through our skin. We are drinking impure water, regardless of its source. **Tap water is susceptible to chemical dumping, run off fertilizers, pesticides, herbicides, raw sewage leakage,**

Tap water is susceptible to chemical dumping, run off fertilizers, pesticides, herbicides, raw sewage leakage, hormones, heavy metals, parasites, arsenic, radon, chlorine and more.

The American diet consists primarily of acid forming foods.

hormones, heavy metals, parasites, arsenic, radon, chlorine and more. Bottled water and Reverse Osmosis have capitalized on our impure tap water, yet both of these are not providing the healthy hydration we require. Why?

Because 75% of bottled water is more acidic than tap water, and 25% of all bottled water is nothing more than untreated tap water.

A recent study on bottled water found that 33% violated industry standards with high levels of synthetic organic chemicals, bacteria, and arsenic. Perhaps the worst offense is the leaching of petro-chemicals from the plastic into the bottled water which has proven to contribute to certain types of breast cancer.

Reverse osmosis and distilled water create highly oxidizing, acidic water devoid of minerals. The bottom line is we are drinking acidic, toxic water with a structure of large molecule clusters that have difficulty penetrating the walls of our cells. The little water we do absorb is unhealthy, and we remain chronically dehydrated. And chronic dehydration over time results in disease.

Our bodies are composed of roughly 70 trillion cells which are 76%-98% water. The health of these cells depends on the quality of the water we drink. Clean, alkaline, micro-clustered water is easily absorbed by our cells, nourishing our cells with mineral nutrients and cleansing our cells of cellular acidic waste. Drinking alkaline water restores our bodies to the proper, healthy pH balance wherein disease cannot flourish.

An acidic environment creates oxidation which makes us age prematurely. Oxidation is a systematic break down of our bodies resulting in wrinkles, degeneration of the bones, organs, glandular systems, cellular membranes, and an overall loss of vitality. You can pop all the anti-oxidant vitamins you want, but it cannot compare to nourishing and cleansing your cells with alkaline rich water.

Drinking the "right" water is the single most important element if you want to achieve and maintain optimal health. The right water is produced, apart from glacier melt, from an alkaline water ionizer. **The ionization process replaces water soluble acids with vital minerals and nutrients, creates a true anti-oxidant, micro-clustered water, aids in the elimination of acids, and super charges the cells in cleansing.**

75% of bottled water is more acidic than tap water, and 25% of all bottled water is nothing more than untreated tap water.

Reverse osmosis and distilled water create highly oxidizing, acidic water devoid of minerals.

Drinking the "right" water is the single most important element if you want to achieve and maintain optimal health.

Alkaline water is a powerful natural antioxidant.

For centuries, human beings have enjoyed the benefits of chemical-free, pure, natural water flowing in streams fed by glaciers; alkalization of water through ionization brings the goodness of this glacial water to your kitchen.

Alkaline water (aka ionized water) is electronically enhanced to improve its hydration value. In the ionization process, water is passed over high voltage negative and positive electrodes that separate water into acidic and alkaline.

The 70% alkaline water and 30% acidic water is produced simultaneously in an ionizer. Ionized water is used for cooking and drinking and has significant preventative health benefits. The extra hydroxyl ion in alkaline water helps to carry more oxygen to the cells replenishing them. **Oxidization is the process of aging; an example of oxidization in nature is the rusting of iron. In the human body, oxidization refers to the free radical damage.** These free radicals are oxygen atoms that have been rendered unstable due to the loss of an electron. Pollution, stress, unhealthy eating habits can increase the amount of free radicals in the body. Ionized water has the same antioxidant properties as fresh raw fruits and vegetables.

As we get older our body's natural ability to produce antioxidants weakens. Free radicals can damage vital cells causing several acute and chronic ailments such as cancer, Alzheimer's disease, atherosclerosis, and rheumatoid arthritis; the onset of these ailments can be prevented through the antioxidant properties of alkaline water.

Alkaline water also helps to delay the appearance of the visible signs of aging. It helps to reduce wrinkles and preserves the natural radiance and glow of the skin. Antioxidants are also known to slow the progression of age related macular degeneration.

Since alkalization of water not only makes it a powerful antioxidant, but also increases its hydration value, it can be used to prevent heart burn. **More than an illness, heart burn is often the physical signal of dehydration in the gastrointestinal tract and the esophagus.** It is essential to hydrate these parts of the digestive system to ensure digestive health.

The continuous dehydration of these organs can cause several health issues such as cancers of the gastrointestinal tract, ulcers, and even

---

Alkaline water (aka ionized water) is electronically enhanced to improve its hydration value.

The extra hydroxyl ion in alkaline water helps to carry more oxygen to the cells replenishing them.

hernias. Since ionized water has improved hydrating properties, it can help to hydrate the digestive tract better than plain tap water.

Alkaline water can also be used to reduce instances of back pain. Dehydration of the spinal discs is often the primary cause of back pain, an ailment that afflicts million of Americans. If you do not suffer from spinal damage or muscular problems, back pain should be attributed to the dehydration of these discs that act as a cushion between the vertebras

Most people experience immediate benefits from the consumption of ionized alkaline water. Among these benefits is the reduction in instances of headaches and migraine. Since alkaline water helps to better hydrate the tissues and muscles in the eyes and the brain, it can be used as a natural remedy for migraine.

Angina is a chronic condition that can be life threatening if not controlled in time. Also known as intense chest pain, the condition is often a result of the dehydration in the lung and heart axis. While it is recommended that you take prescribed medication to control this incredibly painful condition, drinking ionized alkaline water can help to remedy the problem over time.

One of the keys to a long and healthy life is the supply of great quality water.

Ionizing water systems present an excellent method to fulfill this necessity by generating high quality water of varying pH levels. Water of differing pH values can be used in a variety of useful ways to maximize our well-being and also the condition of our natural environment. We check out just how these water ionizers help to improve the health of our living environment and ultimately our own personal health.

In order for the body to function correctly a continual intake of good quality water is a necessity. **Numerous research indicates that the daily consumption of the right amount of water can drastically reduce the occurrence of migraines and headaches, joint pain, lower back pain, along with arthritis.** Drinking the required two to three ltrs. of water each day helps continue to keep skin thoroughly hydrated, betters skin tone, muscle definition, and also improves the metabolic process assisting in weight-loss.

> Most people experience immediate benefits from the consumption of ionized alkaline water. Among these benefits is the reduction in instances of headaches and migraine.

> In order for the body to function correctly a continual intake of good quality water is a necessity.

Alkaline ionized water carries 2 powerful anti-oxidant benefits for your body.

This type of water has a negative charge that can be calculated in millivolts (mV). This denotes the amount of Oxygen Reduction Potential (ORP) that the water has. Generally speaking, the lower this ORP amount the higher the potential for the water to reduce unfavorable oxidation in the body. In addition, this type of water contains hydroxyl ions. Negatively charged hydroxy ions composed of one hydrogen atom and an oxygen atom (HO-) hold an additional electron that is used to easily neutralize positively charged, damaging free radicals before they can harm healthy cells.

Slightly to moderately acidic water has shown to be very effective in maintaining the skin in a proper balanced, healthy state. Washing with acidic water with a pH value of anywhere between 5.0 and 6.0 is a great way to improve the tone and firmness of your skin for a more even, vibrant complexion. It works as a natural astringent, getting rid of dirt and oil without the use of chemicals and additives that are abundant in cosmetic products these days and also tightens pores for smooth silky skin. Acidic water is also recognized to help reduce a bunch of skin conditions including, pimples and acne, fungus type infections as in athletes foot and nail fungus, and dry itchy skin conditions associated with eczema and psoriasis. Acidic water is also really beneficial for the scalp and can easily alleviate dry itchy conditions, dermatitis, and dandruff. This water moreover makes a great germ zapping mouth wash, gargle and plaque remover free of the use of potentially hazardous chemicals.

By all standards, much of our drinking water today contains chemicals detrimental to health.

Federal, state, city laws, and guidelines govern levels of chemicals permitted in municipal water. Ironically, one of the deadly chemicals, chlorine, is introduced out of necessity to kill things that would be of even greater consequence. Common knowledge and reason should lead each of us to action to ensure within our home's chlorine, thrihalomethanes, and other harmful chemicals are not permitted to pass from tap to glass. For over 20 years I personally have not consumed municipal water unprotected except for when dining outside our home, but I am continually surprised to learn of friends and acquaintances who have not applied much thought or action to this rather apparent water problem. Whether individuals give regard that water is contaminated is the obvious.

> Generally speaking, the lower this ORP amount the higher the potential for the water to reduce unfavorable oxidation in the body.

> Common knowledge and reason should lead each of us to action to ensure within our home's chlorine, thrihalomethanes, and other harmful chemicals are not permitted to pass from tap to glass.

170

Are You Eating Enough Alkaline Foods?

The list of Alkaline and Acidic foods can be a great help. But even when one knows better, it is hard because an Alkaline diet is generally not that of convenience or preference.

Alkalizing foods include dark greens like spinach, vegetables like celery and cabbage, fruits like apricot and avocado, and other foods that are not so likely to magically appear on the "random" menu. Selecting the alkaline foods is only half the equation — avoiding the acidic foods is also important. But even if one were to master the choice of alkaline foods, the challenge is greater than first appears, and for good reason. Just as our bodies are 70% water, so our diet consists in considerable proportion of water. So, does water help a serious seeker of the Alkaline Diet?

Aha... here's where the bigger challenge — and perhaps surprise — lies.

A very real pH dilemma for many of us is that try as one may to eat alkaline foods, nearly all of the drinking water most people have access to is NOT alkaline. Rather it is acidic. Perhaps some folks who test their water will find it to be neutral or weakly alkaline, but the vast majority of drinking water tests Acidic.

Good thing we keep soda drinks in the fridge! Right?

Because certainly a nice "soda" drink ought to be less acidic than acidic tap water.

Wouldn't it be? NO!

Soda pop is one of the worst offenders on the pH scale of Human Health. Acid Acid Acid.

Bottled Water to the rescue then. What else is there to look to for the solution? The plain fact is that of the tests I have seen data on for Bottled Water... you guessed right... Acidic. Even water prepared by Reverse Osmosis. So our list of options to find Alkaline water is "drying up" — pardon the pun.

What is the consequence to our health of our Acidic diet and our Acidic water and our Acidic soda drinks? Can't our bodies accommodate the pH of what we drink? That is a fabulous question. It is a complicated

A very real pH dilemma for many of us is that try as one may to eat alkaline foods, nearly all of the drinking water most people have access to is NOT alkaline. Rather it is acidic.

question. But in a few words let me share some perspective. **Your body consisting of trillions of cells is one of incredible design and YES — it does have provisions for accommodating a wide range of environmental and dietary parameters. But it must regulate body processes within very narrowly defined parameters.** In order to accommodate the wide rage of inputs while maintaining the narrowly governed body function metrics, it must prioritize and sometimes must sacrifice one good thing for a better.

> The pH of your blood, for example, must be 7.2 to 7.4 — a narrowly defined metric.

The pH of your blood, for example, must be 7.2 to 7.4 — a narrowly defined metric. So important to us is our blood pH metric which must be maintained that the body will sacrifice minerals including calcium from our bones in order to preserve our blood pH so we can live another day. But over time, when we stress our body by continuing to impose upon it such great demands for it to solve because of our preferences of diet and water, we will eventually pay the price. Good health is not a given but rather it is something that we must all strive for.

Drinking Acidic water does not help win the fight for Optimal Health.

Solving water pH is accomplished with a Water Ionizer. Ionization accomplishes a very important enhancement to one's drinking water. It actually turns tap water into Antioxidants!

> Change your water and change your health... No success can compensate for the premature failure of the human body, and you are worth whatever it takes to make sure your health is the best it can be.

Hard to believe? But true. Oxidation Reduction Potential (ORP) is a measurement of Antioxidant value, and the higher the positive ORP the worse something is for our body while the lower or more negative the ORP the better something is for us in terms of Antioxidant potential. **Your health is in part a function of what you ingest. So the question for each of us is whether we will apply some "basic" (pardon the pun) knowledge of science and health and take action to solve our personal water crisis before the water we drink gets the better of us.** They say that what we eat becomes what we are. With 70% of our body water, I propose we justifiably state we also are what we drink. Change your water and change your health... No success can compensate for the premature failure of the human body, and you are worth whatever it takes to make sure your health is the best it can be.

Pure, clean, alkaline water has become such a concern that it is estimated that 50 percent of us now drink bottled water. In fact, we now pay more for it than we do gasoline. But be aware, The Natural Resources

Defense Council (NRDC) conducted a four-year study on 103 brands of bottled water and found that one-third of those brands contained synthetic and organic chemicals and bacteria, making them unsafe for human consumption. The council reported that one brand, labeled "spring water," actually came from an industrial parking lot near a hazardous waste site.

In a recent year, the Environmental Protection agency reported 82,000 violations of safe drinking water standards affecting more than 78 million Americans. Don't assume that if your home's tap water looks, tastes, and smells OK that it is safe.

Many of the most dangerous contaminants cannot be detected with your senses. Dr. Joseph Price, author of "Coronaries, Cholesterol and Chlorine", believes there is a strong correlation between chlorine being introduced into our water supply in 1904 and our present epidemic of heart disease, cancer, and senility.

"The basic cause of arteriosclerosis, heart attacks, and most forms of stroke is... the chlorine in processed water," he writes.

Plenty of alkaline water is the key to overall good health, along with quality supplements that your body can absorb. After all, your body is 70% water and your blood even more at 94%. Learn where to obtain pure, healthy, alkaline water.

Alkaline water has also been found to be highly effective in relieving the symptoms of diabetes and helping sufferers get off their medication... but before taking any steps on your own it's important to seek a diagnosis from a qualified physician.

In Type 1 diabetes, the symptoms can often come on suddenly and dramatically. It mostly shows up in childhood or early teens often after an illness, virus, or injury. The extra stress can cause diabetic ketoacidosis. Without treatment, ketoacidosis can lead to coma and death. Symptoms of Type 2 diabetes are often not obvious and you may think they are due to aging or obesity. **It's possible to have Diabetes 2 for many years without being aware that you have it.** Steroids and stress can be big factors in the onset of Diabetes 2. It's important to take this illness seriously; it can lead to unpleasant outcomes like blindness, kidney failure, heart disease, and nerve damage.

Many of the most dangerous contaminants cannot be detected with your senses.

It's important to take diabetes seriously; it can lead to unpleasant outcomes like blindness, kidney failure, heart disease, and nerve damage.

Here are some of the Common symptoms of Diabetes 1 and Diabetes 2

Excessive and Unusual Tiredness:

When you contract diabetes the body is mostly unable to use glucose for fuel. It begins instead to metabolize fat to get the extra fuel it needs. This process is not very efficient. You have less energy than before and you feel tired.

Weight Loss You Just Can't Explain:

Because you can't metabolize sugar, much of the fuel in your food is excreted in your urine via the kidneys. You may find yourself eating way more food than normal and still losing weight. You become dehydrated and lose even more weight.

Excessive thirst:

The high concentration of sugar in your bloodstream overcomes your normal kidney function. Instead of being re-absorbed for future use the sugar is passed out in your urine. The brain senses a need to dilute the blood and you experience this as thirst. As a result you find yourself drinking more water as the body tries to correct this sugar imbalance.

Increased Urination:

The body tries to excrete the excess sugar via the kidneys. As a result you pass more water and feel thirsty.

Overeating:

The body will try to increase its levels of insulin production to reduce the excess blood sugar. Insulin is the key that opens the muscles and lean tissue to receive the sugar. But in Type 2 Diabetes you become insulin resistant. Your muscles refuse to take up the sugar.

Another job of insulin is to make you hungry... you can't absorb this extra insulin so you are driven to eat more.

Wounds Refuse to Heal:

When you have high blood sugar levels your white blood cells can't do

---

The high concentration of sugar in your bloodstream overcomes your normal kidney function.

The body will try to increase its levels of insulin production to reduce the excess blood sugar.

Long term diabetes can cause your arteries to thicken, reducing blood flow.

their job properly. As a result your wounds heal slowly and often get infected.

Thickening of the Arteries:

Long term diabetes can cause your arteries to thicken, reducing blood flow.

You catch more Infections:

Because your immune system is no longer functioning as well as it should you'll often find you are contracting skin and yeast infections as well as urinary tract infections.

Mood Swings:

You may find yourself agitated, irritable or unable to concentrate — all are symptoms of very high blood sugar levels

Impaired Vision:

You may find you have difficulty focusing and things appear blurry.

Don't despair! There are natural solutions available. **Alkaline water has been found to be highly effective in relieving the symptoms of diabetes and helping sufferers get off their medication.**

Ordinary tap water can be run through an alkaline water ionizer (like the one we will send to you <u>ABSOLUTELY</u> <u>FREE</u> when you become a Client of our top-level Advertising and Management Service!) and produce both short-term and long-term relief for diabetes sufferers. And this ionized water is rich in negative ions which act as a powerful anti-oxidant to neutralize the hordes of free radicals in our bodies.

The federal, state, and local laws that regulate chemicals levels in public water can only do so much, which is why it is important to know more about alkaline water ionizer.

Helping drinking populations get cleaner, healthier water, the ionizer has various capabilities to keep chlorine and other harmful chemicals from getting into our drinking water. True, chlorine administration in our water is permitted to kill bacteria, the fact remains that chlorine is a lethal

Alkaline water has been found to be highly effective in relieving the symptoms of diabetes and helping sufferers get off their medication.

Having an ionizer at home saves families from potential dangers brought about by unhealthy drinking water.

substance. **Having an ionizer at home saves families from potential dangers brought about by unhealthy drinking water.**

In the recent news, water systems all over the United States have been proven tainted with prescription medications, an alarming fact considering the dangers such drugs could do to the drinking public. It has been known also that many tributaries to major river systems all over the United States carry dumped waste. Even more alarming is that many water treatment plants are not equipped with facilities that could eliminate such seepage into the peoples' daily dose of water. **With an alkaline water ionizer at home, families are assured that they are drinking clean, uncontaminated water.**

Today, many forms and types of water ionizer appliances have come out to provide households with cleaner drinking water, among them the alkaline water ionizer. While there are stated claims that antioxidants in water are eradicated with this home appliance, its equal advantage is eliminating free radicals and sanitizing food products by neutralizing this acid condition. Thus, there results a healthy alkaline balance in your body.

It's never too late to start living healthier and using a water ionizer. As against continued drinking of water where dangerous contaminants, lethal substances and harmful bacteria are present, drinking water that runs through an alkaline water ionizer eliminates your body from damages and gives everyone in your family a cleaner, healthier living.

What is the main characteristic of Alkaline Water that makes it good for your health? The answer is a negative ORP or Oxidation Reduction Potential.

So what's ORP? And how can it help you? Read on...

When we see a piece of iron rusting or a slice of apple turning brown, we are looking at examples of relatively slow oxidation. When we look at a fire, we are witnessing an example of rapid oxidation. We now know that oxidation involves an exchange of electrons between two atoms. The atom that loses an electron in the process is said to be "oxidized." The one that gains an electron is said to be "reduced." In picking up that extra electron, it loses the electrical energy that makes it "hungry" for more electrons. Thus we get the term Oxidation (losing an electron) Reduction (gaining an electron) Potential. The potential of a given substance to take or leave electrons is very important. If you consistently drink water with a high

---

Drinking water that runs through an alkaline water ionizer eliminates your body from damages and gives everyone in your family a cleaner, healthier living.

positive ORP or Oxidation Reduction Potential, the water will have a tendency to steal electrons from the other atoms in your body, oxidizing your other atoms.

Remember the examples above of iron rusting and an apple turning brown. Basically that is what water with a high ORP will do to you.

Remember that oxidation causes decay.

Examples of drinks with a high positive ORP are coffee, soda, bottled water, Gatorade and Powerade, and almost every drink sold at stores. Even tap water has a high ORP even though it is required by law to have a neutral pH level.

If you consistently drink water with a high negative ORP or Oxidation Reduction Potential, the water will have a tendency to leave electrons with atoms in your body that are in need of them. The water will basically reduce the atoms that are missing electrons so that those atoms and molecules do not oxidize your body. Again, remember that oxidation causes decay. You do not want that.

The only water that I am aware of that has a high negative ORP is alkaline water, usually produced by a special water ionizer. Alkaline Water can virtually reverse the negative effects of all of the oxidizing drinks and foods that we eat daily.

An anti-oxidant is a substance that has a high negative ORP or Oxidation Reduction Potential.

You may have also heard of the term anti-oxidant. **Simply stated an anti-oxidant is a substance that has a high negative ORP or Oxidation Reduction Potential.** There is a huge market for anti-oxidants because they help prevent your body from decaying and oxidizing.

THE BEST ANTI-OXIDANT AVAILABLE IS ALKALINE WATER.

Acidic properties are often found in tap water.

If you have looked into any variety of non-acidity diets, you may already know the many benefits of maintaining an alkaline state inside your body. Just the increased energy levels and greater sense of well being is enough for most people to see the value of limiting things that create acidity internally, but have you ever thought about what water does to your body?

If you assumed it is literally nothing and has no effect, you might be surprised to learn that acidic properties are often found in tap water.

If you are trying to drink more water in order to abide by an alkaline diet or simply want to know more about establishing a healthy body that functions properly and feels great every day, it is in your best interest to learn a bit more about what purified water can actually do for your body.

Water is good for us and, as a matter of fact, we are supposed to drink at least 8 glasses of water every day to keep ourselves hydrated and healthy. However not all water is the same and some have more benefits than others, such as drinking alkaline water.

First of all, drinking alkaline water can make us look younger because this water type keeps the skin hydrated. The reason is that the ionized water has various smaller clusters containing it. **Alkaline water also has the benefit of aiding digestion since it helps to produce extra saliva which carries the food down to the digestive tract.** You should also eat food with more fiber in it as the saliva works together with the fiber in the stomach to help get rid of toxic wastes from the body and enhance the metabolism.

It is also a good anti-aging agent due to the effect of ionized water that has many antioxidants in it. The antioxidants are helping the body by getting rid of harmful free radicals that are basically a major cause of aging.

In addition it helps with weight loss since, first of all, drinking water regularly makes one eat less by curbing that constant hunger. **Also the metabolism is effectively increased so that helps with burning the calories faster in the body.**

It is a great detoxificator since with drinking plenty of water, the toxins from the body get flushed out, especially when it comes to the kidneys. Sadly with age the kidneys are less equipped to do it on their own so they need outside help to perform their job the optimal way.

Alkaline water also helps with minimizing the risk of various heart diseases such as heart attacks. **Just by increasing the intake of fresh liquid, people are less prone to get heart attacks in their lives.** These are just some of the benefits of consuming fresh, pure, and alkaline water. By picking up a glass and drinking more often you increase your health benefits and get to live longer as well.

Scientists and researchers are making much debate over the past few years about the quality of the water that is being consumed worldwide. Many experts also have believed and concluded that **low-quality tap water can cause many health hazards.** And so people started drinking mineral water

> Alkaline water is a great detoxificator since with drinking plenty of water, the toxins from the body get flushed out, especially when it comes to the kidneys.

> Alkaline water also helps with minimizing the risk of various heart diseases such as heart attacks.

instead of tap water. In recent times the primary concern of a consumer: "Is mineral water safe to consume?"

An individual on an average is advised to consume 2.5 liters to 4 liters of water every day to improve the overall health. It is for sure that the quality of the water cannot be compromised, thought there are different versions about the merit and demerit of the alkaline water. However, one thing for sure is that by making the water alkaline, it helps improve the purity of the water. Alkaline water helps in neutralizing the acids and toxins from the body. Ionized alkaline water is considered to be a great detoxifier that helps cleanse the system.

Every system requires water to maintain a correct acid-alkaline balance. The quality of water plays a vital role in maintaining the overall health of an individual. Water that is consumed must be able to flush and prevent toxins and chemicals that get accumulated in the system. It should also transport vitamins and minerals to the cells of the body to improve the metabolic rate and to flush out dead cells. This is what Alkaline water does best.

The benefits of the alkaline water involves in neutralizing the acids and toxins in the system. **As the acids and the toxins are nullified the body will now be able to remove them from the system.** A study has proved that ionized water acts like a conductor of electrochemical activity from cell to cells. Alkaline water also helps resist the disease, and the process of aging is slowed down by increasing the intercellular hydration. The other benefits of consuming alkaline water includes replenishing essential minerals, stabilizing and protecting cells, maintaining a normal blood flow and acid-alkaline balance, flushing out and preventing waste from accumulating in cells, and preventing free radicals.

Free radicals are nothing but positively charged oxygen atoms. These atoms are created by the body for the purpose of oxidizing putrefactive substances. But when these oxygen atoms are produced they tend to steal the electrons from the stable cells. **When a healthy cell looses an electron it becomes weak and dies. By consuming ionized alkaline water, cells losing the electrons are prevented and the oxygen molecules are reestablished.** This neutralizes the free radicals. When the body is hydrated properly, the thirst for the water increases and the body's craving for food decreases simultaneously. A study has concluded that the body's cry for food is actually the need for water. Health, both inside and outside can be

Alkaline water helps in neutralizing the acids and toxins from the body.

The other benefits of consuming alkaline water includes replenishing essential minerals, stabilizing and protecting cells, maintaining a normal blood flow and acid-alkaline balance, flushing out and preventing waste from accumulating in cells, and preventing free radicals.

achieved by consuming alkaline ionized water.

And now you can drink all the alkaline ionized water you want... <u>for</u> <u>free</u>!

Just go to the LAST SECTION of this book to discover how we can help you make money and restore your pH balance. As you'll see, our Advertising and Management Service is a powerful and proven way you can stay home and make money. **Best of all, we do it all for you while you sit back and collect a percentage of all the sales we make for you!** Please read the next section carefully to discover how all this works. As you'll see, **you can get a <u>FREE</u> WATER IONIZER just for becoming a Client!** Flip the page and read on...

SECTION FOUR:

How to Make Huge Sums of Money in the $28 Billion Dollar Health Supplement Industry... Without Lifting a Single Finger!

How to Make Huge Sums of Money in the $28 Billion Dollar Health Supplement Industry... Without Lifting a Single Finger!

THANK YOU for taking the time to go through this book.

If you skimmed through Section One this book and read some of the articles, then you know **why I call EXCESSIVE BODY ACIDITY (E.B.A.) 'The Silent Killer that may be slowly killing you right now."** That's just my opinion. But it's based on all of the research you read about in the first section of this book. And in the Second Section, you read about the dangers of too much sugar. As you have seen, **I call SUGAR 'The Deadliest Acid?"** I call it this because #1: I really do believe that it may be the deadliest acid of them all, and is very dangerous. #2: Again, I have used the *question mark* in my description for the reasons I told you about in my Introduction. Then in the Third Section, you learned about the major health benefits of drinking pure alkaline ionized water.

Let me remind you again that I am NOT a doctor or health practitioner. I am simply a man who CARES DEEPLY about his health and wants to do all I can to live longer, feel better, have more energy and vitality and not suffer from all of the DEADLY DISEASES that kill so many others. I'm betting that these are the same things that you want, too. This research that my assistant and I did on E.B.A. was SHOCKING to both of us and I'm betting that you feel the same way.

And as I also told you in my Introduction: I may not be a medical doctor or an expert in health and nutrition…

But I have become an expert in business and marketing.

My wife Eileen and I started our Direct-Response Marketing company in 1988 with a few hundred dollars and have parlayed it into a multi million dollar corporation. **Since that time, we have generated many tens of millions of dollars from our headquarters in the tiny town of Goessel,**

Kansas. We have discovered many little-known marketing methods for making huge sums of money. **And I'm ALWAYS on the lookout for new products, services and opportunities to make ourselves and our Clients more money.**

And that brings me to the next important subject and the theme of this entire Section:

How you can make more money!

Our advertising and management service is a proven way to make money.

This works like an expensive franchise...

When you buy an expensive franchise, you are getting these three things:

1. A proven opportunity that has been time-tested in every way.

2. Insider secrets from experts who understand every aspect of this business.

3. Ongoing help, support, and guidance from these experts — anytime you want it.

Those are the three main reasons why people pay tens of thousands of dollars for a franchise. And each one of those things can help you make enormous sums of money.

And yet, the average franchise is expensive.

Very expensive.

Just go on the Internet and spend a little time looking at all the franchises for sale. You'll see. These franchises can sell for $30,000.00 to $50,000.00 or much, much more. It's not uncommon to spend hundreds of thousands of dollars on a franchise. In some cases, you could actually spend millions of dollars.

And yet, people are more than willing to go to the bank and borrow tens or hundreds of thousands of dollars for a high-dollar franchise, because they want the three main benefits;

#1: They want a proven opportunity that is making other people money right now.

#2: They want ALL of the inside secrets from experts who are already making money in this business.

#3: They want the ongoing help, support, and guidance from experts who will be there for them every step of the way.

Listen, business can be very risky and there are many things that can go wrong. It's very easy to lose all of your money in business. In fact, according to the U.S. Department of Commerce, over 95% of all of the small businesses that are started this month will be out of business in just 5 years.

That's a 95% failure rate!

And yet, according to our research, a franchise is almost the opposite of this. It has a 85% SUCCESS RATE! That means that an average of 85 out of 100 of the franchises that are started this month will still be in business in 5 years.

> So now you know: You can start a regular business and have a 95% chance of failure. Or you can invest in a franchise and have a 85% chance of success!

When you look at those statistics, it's easy to see WHY so many people are willing to go to the bank and take out a second or third mortgage on their home and go DEEPLY IN DEBT in order to have their own franchise. They know that the minute they do this that they have a 85% chance of success, versus a 95% chance of failure.

And yet, there are many people who don't have tens or hundreds of thousands of dollars and can't get a loan, but still want to make a lot of money. What do those people do?

Well, they have a few basic choices:

A. They can start some kind of low cost service business that is dirt-cheap to get into. (This is what I did back in 1985, when I started my first business.)

B. They can get involved in some kind of low cost dealership or multi-level marketing opportunity. (I joined over a DOZEN of these companies when I was dirt-poor, but wanted to make a lot of money.)

C. They can get involved in various Direct-Response and/or Internet Marketing related business opportunities that can be very inexpensive to start.

Let me take a minute to talk about these low cost options:

OPTION #1: Starting your own service business.

I started my first business back in 1985. It was a carpet and upholstery cleaning business. I began this company with my best friend, Gary, with just a few hundred dollars and a beat up van and equipment that we made payments on. We made money immediately because BOTH of us were salespeople, and because I had worked as a carpet cleaner with a national franchise and my boss had sent me to carpet cleaning school.

So even though we did not buy a franchise, I had been working for a national carpet and upholstery cleaning company and was trained by them so I knew what I was doing and quickly taught Gary everything I knew. And we were both very aggressive salespeople who were not afraid to…

Knock on as many as 200 doors a day!

Yes, there were many days that Gary and I would spend the entire day knocking on as many as 200 doors... passing out our fliers... and trying to get inside people's homes so we could give them a free bid... We worked very hard, delivered hundreds of 'sales pitches' a month and achieved success, but only because I had gone to Waco, Texas, and attended a 2 week carpet and upholstery cleaning school (that my boss paid for) and because Gary and I were very aggressive salespeople who delivered hundreds of sales presentations a month.

And if you want to succeed in your own service business you must also have these two things: First, you must have prior knowledge and experience in the service business you want to get involved in and, second, you must be willing to be a very aggressive salesperson or hire somebody who is…

There is no other way that I know of.

There are many different service businesses you can get involved in. But just doing good work is NOT enough. **You have to get out there and hustle.** And yet, if you have the knowledge and experience and you're willing to do knock on a lot of doors and deliver dozens of sales presentations a month, then you can achieve great success. **There are many different service businesses that can be started dirt-cheap.** Just get out there and start selling! And speaking of selling, your next LOW COST BUSINESS OPTION involves a lot of selling…

OPTION #2: Joining a network marketing company.

I have a love/hate relationship with network marketing. On one hand, I love it because it has helped so many average people who could NEVER afford a regular business. I am one of these people. Before I began my carpet and upholstery cleaning business in 1985, I had already joined many different network marketing companies. I never made any money and, yet, my experience with this type of business opportunity lead me to starting my 'real business' in 1985.

The truth is: **Network Marketing is very much a 'REAL BUSINESS' and, yet, the majority of people who are involved in these types of opportunities do NOT treat it as if it is a real business.** And of the small group who do take it seriously and work hard at it, many of them do not have the help, support, and guidance of experienced leaders and experts who help them every step of the way. Thank goodness there are exceptions to this and…

Many of those people are making HUGE SUMS OF MONEY!

Yet, to make money in Network Marketing, you must understand that it's <u>NOT</u> a get-rich-quick opportunity, or a hobby, or social club, or a chance to sit back and make money from the efforts of other people.

And that's one of the reasons that I HATE NETWORK MARKETING!

Yes, as much as I **love** the people who are involved in network marketing and love the fact that it does let average people start their own businesses for very little money, I also **HATE** Network Marketing because it misleads people into thinking that it's a fast, simple, and easy way to get super rich in no time flat.

It's neither of those things.

So many people (myself included) get started in Network Marketing with the idea that it's a fast, simple, and easy way to get rich. We soon find out that it's neither one of those things and we become very discouraged and quit. And even though we quit, the Network Marketing companies and the

187

top-level distributors (called 'Heavy Hitters') make huge sums of money from all the people who come and go. Yes, they make huge sums of money on all of the distributors who give up and quit after a few months or years.

The bottom line:

While the average distributor NEVER makes any substantial sum of money, the Network Marketing companies always do.

These Network Marketing companies are like the casinos in Las Vegas, Reno, or Atlantic City... Most of the people who gamble in those casinos make little or no money. Huge numbers of people leave Las Vegas with less money than they had when they arrived and, therefore, the casinos are making all of their money on the 'losers' and not the 'winners.'

And there are always more losers than winners.

The same thing happens in the Network Marketing industry every year. Just like there are 'winners' who leave Las Vegas with millions, there are a small group of people at the top of every Network Marketing company who make hundreds of thousands of dollars a year. **And yet, the bulk of distributors are making very little or even no money.**

The Network Marketing companies make HUGE PROFITS on the larger group of distributors who NEVER QUALIFY to receive all of the commissions that the small group of 'heavy hitters' receive... And while all of this is fully legal, it's immoral to convince people that it's 'fast, simple, and easy' to make a lot of money in Network Marketing. It's not.

Like every business, Network Marketing requires a significant investment of time, money, and expertise to rise to the top. If you want to get rich in this business, you must learn how to recruit huge numbers of distributors to become part of your sales organization.

There's NO OTHER WAY...

And if you don't have the sales and marketing experience to do this, or if you don't want to acquire the knowledge and skills necessary to become a sales and marketing expert, then your chances of making any substantial sum of money are slim to none. I have more to say about Network Marketing later, but first, let's move on to the 3rd and final way that you can turn small sums of money into a substantial sum of monthly income...

OPTION #3: You can get involved in various Direct-Response and/or Internet Marketing related business opportunities that can be very inexpensive to start.

Direct-Response Marketing is the type of business that made my wife, Eileen and me INSTANT MILLIONAIRES. We started in September of 1988 with only $300.00 and quickly turned it into a total revenue of over $10,000,000.00 in our first five years.

Yes, we went from a few hundred dollars to over ten million dollars in less than five years! And that was just the start of our success.

Within our first 19 years, we had generated a grand total of over $100,000,000.00 and we're still going strong. I say none of this to brag or show off. I hate it when people try to brag about all of the money they make and I'm sure you feel the same way. No, the only reason I tell you about our phenomenal rags-to-riches success in Direct-Response Marketing is because **it is ABSOLUTE PROOF that this is the type of business that can make you very rich in a fast period of time...** Let me tell you a little more about our story and prove to you that this type of business really does have the power to make you enormous sums of money...

OUR STORY.

Eileen and I started our Direct-Response Marketing business with only $300.00 because THAT WAS ALL THE MONEY WE HAD at the time... Back then, we were in the carpet cleaning business and coming up with more than a few hundred dollars to invest in any new business was IMPOSSIBLE for us to do... But we did manage to scrape together $300.00 by selling one of our carpet cleaning vans (a 1985 Chevy Van who's engine only ran on 5 of it's 6 cylinders) for a few hundred dollars. We used this money to run two small ads in a couple of national publications. **We ran the ads (which sold a small book that I wrote) and then sat back to see what would happen.**

WE GOT LUCKY AND THE ADS WERE A HIT!

We got lucky because our little ads made money right away. And we used the money from those 2 ads to buy 2 more ads, and then 4... and 8... and 16, etc. Those little ads kept making a nice profit and within six months, we were bringing in MORE MONEY than we had ever made in our entire lives: an average $500.00 a day.

It's true: **Our small investment of a few hundred dollars soon turned into a thriving small... business that was generating around $16,000.00 a month... and all within six months from the time we got started!**

Eileen and I were on top of the world!

After all...

What other business can you start for a few hundred dollars and then turn it into an average of $500.00 a day within six months? NONE THAT I KNOW OF!!! And this was SEVEN LONG YEARS before the 'World Wide Web' (w.w.w.) caused the Internet to EXPLODE WITH GROWTH!

Yes, today it can be even faster, easier, and cheaper to start a Direct-Response Business thanks to the power of the Internet!

More on that in a moment... But first let me tell you a little more about how we made our fortune. **The more you understand the 'secret of our success,' the more you'll see how this powerful form of marketing can be worth enormous sums of money to you.**

Let's continue... As you know, Eileen and I turned our $300.00 investment into an average of $16,000.00 a month within just six months from the time we started.

And then something happened in the winter of 1989 that made us INSTANT MILLIONAIRES!

Here's what happened: One cold winter morning, I was walking to our mailbox to pull out the mail and in with all of the daily orders was a letter from a marketing consultant from El Cajon, California, named Russ von Hoelscher.

Russ sent a brochure about his consulting services, along with a small note that said, "I've seen your materials and I like what you're doing. I think I can help you make a lot more money. Please give me a call." SO I DID — AND OUR LIVES HAVE NEVER BEEN THE SAME! I simply picked up the phone and called Russ von Hoelscher.

After just a few minutes, I knew that we had to hire him!

So we did. And to make a long story short, **Russ became our personal 'marketing coach' and mentor.** At that time, Russ had over 20 years of experience in Direct-Response Marketing (which was called 'The MAIL ORDER BUSINESS' back then). He went to work to teach us everything that he had learned over the past two decades.

We soaked it all up like a sponge!

Eileen and I were so ambitious and hungry to learn… and **the more Russ taught us, the more we had to know!** We were eager students and we did everything Russ told us to do. And to make a long story, short, thanks to the help, support, and ongoing guidance that we received from Russ von Hoelscher, **we went from bringing in an average of $16,000.00 a month, to… generating a grand total of almost $100,000.00 A WEEK!**

When we hired Russ to become our marketing consultant we were bringing in an average of $16,000.00 a month, and suddenly, (thanks to the fact that Russ knew exactly what to do an how to do it and the fact that we did everything he told us to do) we were bringing in almost $100,000.00 A WEEK! And the best part, all of this took place in just 9 months!

Yes, we went from a total of $16,000.00 a month to almost $100,000.00 a week — in just 9 months! That's the power of working with a true expert who had developed an intimate understanding of this powerful type of business.

Russ had over two decades of accumulated knowledge and experience when we began working with him. He knew exactly what to do and how to do it. He had already made all of the mistakes. **He was able to help us avoid all of the mistakes that DESTROY so many others…** And he taught us how to take advantage of all of the opportunities that we available to us. It would have taken us MANY YEARS to discover all of this on our own.

But Russ helped us get rich, by giving us the two things you'll find in a high-dollar franchise opportunity:

#1: He gave us all of the insider secrets.

Nothing was held back from us. Russ told us exactly what to do and how to do it. He introduced us to all of his most cherished insider contacts. He showed us all of the little-known ways to get rich in this exciting business. He told us all the pitfalls to avoid. **He showed us how to cash-in on the advanced marketing strategies that would have taken us many years to discover on our own.** And he helped steer us clear of all of the MAJOR MISTAKES that caused so many others to go out of business.

These are the same types of things that we would have received with if we had invested in a high-dollar franchise opportunity. But that's not all. He also gave us something else that was equally as valuable…

#2: He gave us the ongoing help, support, and guidance.

These are things that we would have also received if we had invested in an expensive franchise.

Russ was there for us every step of the way. Whenever we had any problem that we didn't know how to solve on our own, we simply picked up the phone and called him. He became our friend and mentor in the business. **He did all kinds of things to look out for us and take us under his wing…** And he was there for us, giving us his knowledge, experience, and wisdom, every time we needed it.…

All of this ultimately helped us generate a total of over $10,000,000.00 within our first five years… **And we parlayed that into a grand total of over ONE HUNDRED MILLION DOLLARS in our first 19 years and have never looked back…**

And yet, as I told you earlier, I am not bragging on us or trying to show off and puff ourselves up about all of the money we've made. **Instead, I am bragging on this wonderful… business of Direct-Response Marketing** (which now includes Internet Marketing) and bragging on the EXTREME VALUE of having the right help, support, and ongoing guidance and encouragement from the right experts who have a DEEP UNDERSTANDING of the business and are ready, willing, and able to help you every step of the way. Russ von Hoelscher was that expert for us. He started as our marketing consultant and quickly became our friend and mentor. He has been there for us every step of the way, to guide us, support us, advise us, and encourage us… This has been worth many millions of dollars to us and is the same type of thing that…

Can be worth enormous sums of money to you!

The **Direct-Response Marketing business can be started DIRT CHEAP and can make YOU enormous sums of money, just as it did for us.** It's such an exciting business and, yet, it is FILLED WITH MAJOR PITFALLS that can stop you from making a lot of money. There are many things that can go wrong. And just like Network Marketing, huge numbers of people get started in this type of business only to run into these pitfalls and quit.

Eileen and I got very lucky, because our first ads were an INSTANT HIT in our marketplace. And then we got lucky again, when we met marketing expert, Russ von Hoelscher. And because of our GREAT LUCK (and the fact that we religiously did whatever Russ told us to do and NEVER questioned any of his advice) and because we worked EXTREMELY HARD and put in many 100-hour weeks (which did NOT seem like 'work' for us because we fell in love with this wonderful business and we loved every minute of it!) we became INSTANT MILLIONAIRES in a few short years…

And the same thing could happen to you!

All you need to get rich in this type of business are the following four items:

1. You must have the right kinds of products and services that millions of people desperately want.

2. You must have the very best 'sales materials' to sell these products and services.

3. You must have the right marketing strategy.

   And last, but not least,

4. You must have the ongoing help, support, and guidance of the right experts who will be there to help you every step of the way.

If you have all four of these things, then the question will NOT be: *"Will you make a lot of money?"* NO WAY! The only question will be: *"How much money will you make and how fast will you make it?"* Because…

You will ultimately make huge sums of money… GUARANTEED!

Yes, I absolutely, positively guarantee that if you have ALL FOUR of those ingredients… MIXED TOGETHER in the right way, you will make more money than you've ever dreamed possible. **These are the four ingredients that have generated tens of millions of dollars for our company and many others…**

Yes, right now, as you're reading my words, BILLIONS OF DOLLARS are being made every single month by a wide variety of people and companies who are using the power of Direct-Response and/or Internet Marketing.

This is such a proven way to make money. And all you need to make all the money you've ever dreamed of making are the four main ingredients I just told you about.

Just mix these four things together in the right way and you will never have to worry about money… ever again!

Does that sound too good to be true?

Probably. And yet, the more you think deeply about those four things and understand just how powerful this form of marketing really is, the more you'll see that…

IT'S THE TRUTH!

This really is a powerful form of marketing that can make you more money than you have ever dreamed possible!

My wife, Eileen, and I are living proof that any average person can get super rich in Direct-Response Marketing. We've been bringing in tens of millions of dollars since the early 1990s… And since that time we took all of the knowledge and experience that we received from Russ von Hoelscher to developed our own knowledge, skills, and abilities…

In short, we have discovered all of the little known advanced marketing methods that can turn small sums of money into a huge and growing fortune… And now we have taken ALL of the best-of-the-best of everything we've learned over the years and have put it into our Advertising and Management Service.

Now this unique and totally proven service is ready to make money for you!

This powerful Advertising and Management Service is a revolutionary new way to get your share of the 28 billion dollars that are being spent each year in the booming Dietary Supplement Industry... without lifting a single finger! **EVERYTHING IS DONE FOR YOU!** And this has the power to make you all the money you want and need!

You will cash-in from an exciting secret that has already brought us millions of dollars!

PLUS, you can MAKE A POTENTIAL FORTUNE while we do everything for you.

Yes, the amazing secrets you'll let us do for you HAVE BEEN PROVEN to make massive sums of money.

How much money?

That's the most exciting part! You see...

The dietary supplement industry is EXPLODING! **This generates over $28 BILLION DOLLARS A YEAR from tens of millions of customers who care deeply about their health.** And we have developed an amazing new way to let YOU cash-in from this BOOMING MARKET... without lifting a single finger!

The reason I'm not keeping this opportunity to myself and keeping all the money is because this is a powerful way that we can BOTH get super rich!

I am convinced that this new breakthrough will make many people up to $100,000.00 a year or even more! That's only my STRONG BELIEF, but it's based on some very solid facts.

After all, this is a new way to cash-in on 3 of the most powerful breakthroughs in history.

And my staff and I will do all of the work to make you the maximum money!

This Advertising and Management Service is totally unique in every way.

IT HAS TO BE. WHY? BECAUSE THE TYPE OF MARKETING WE DO FOR YOU — 'DIRECT-RESPONSE MARKETING' — CAN BE VERY COMPLICATED, EXPENSIVE, AND TIME-CONSUMING… You must test many different things. What works one month, may not work the next. **Our experts must stay on top of all these constant changes and keep testing new ways to make money.**

There are many services that will take care of your advertising for you. You give them your money and they advertise your product or service while you sit back and collect the orders.

But this new money-making service is totally different:

Not only do we do all of the advertising for you, but we (along with our partners) also make all the sales, ship all the products, handle all customer service work, and then send you weekly checks for your share of the money!

That's THE FIRST WAY you get paid.

As you'll see...

This has the power to pay you a huge monthly income that can keep coming to you and never stop.

This new discovery lets you cash-in with a proven goldmine that is already generating billions of dollars every year.

The dietary supplement industry is booming!

The GIANT companies in this industry are getting super rich!

And now, with this opportunity…

YOU AND I can GET RICH — the same way these giant corporations make their fortune.

Yes, getting rich is simply finding the right opportunity at the right time and getting involved with the right people and having the right Systems and processes in place so that you can make money automatically.

Now you will have ALL FOUR of these elements in place.

You will be perfectly positioned to make the LARGEST sum of money in the fastest time! And I'll do everything for YOU the same way that our System has done everything for me! **You'll be tapping into the same powerful and proven marketing System that…**

Made me an INSTANT MILLIONAIRE in no time flat.

Yes, as you'll see in a moment — the marketing system for our Advertising and Management Service has already generated many millions of dollars. My wife and I became INSTANT MILLIONAIRES with this amazing System — and we have spent the last two decades perfecting and fine-tuning it to the point to which I can BOLDLY proclaim…

This is the closest you'll ever get to having your own money-machine!

Your timing couldn't be better! Tens of millions of people CARE DEEPLY about their health have NOT heard about the amazing health discoveries that you read about in this book and are the FOUNDATION of our Advertising and Management Service.

And as you'll see, this has the power to make you financially set for life! But there's more! Much, much more. Read on…

Our new Advertising and Management Service was developed to fill a huge and growing gap in the multi-billion dollar business opportunity market.

This gap has created millions of people who would LOVE to make a lot of money, but HATE all of the time, work, risk, and other headaches and hassles that must be done to build and run a successful business.

Our powerful and proven Marketing System will do ALL of the selling and marketing for you, while you sit back and collect the weekly checks! This lets you profit by helping us fill this huge and growing gap in the multi-billion dollar business opportunity market in a whole new way. We do all the work for you and RUSH you a check for your share of all the sales we make.

As you'll see, although nobody can promise or guarantee that you will get paid any specific sum of money, this truly is designed to pay you thousands of dollars a month that come to you like clockwork!

And that brings us to the only problem… WHERE and HOW do you reach these millions of people who care deeply about their health and are searching for this unique opportunity? That answer to that question is coming up next! Read on…

You are now part of a small group who will let our company do all of the advertising and marketing for you to sell our Service to the LARGEST number of people and RUSH you a check for your share of the money!

With this amazing service, **I will build and manage your own DIETARY SUPPLEMENT BUSINESS for you.** My goal is to do all we can to MAKE SURE that you get paid the LARGEST sum of money in the FASTEST time and keep that money coming in like clockwork!

We do all the work and you get paid 3 ways!

YES, WE ALL THE WORK, AND SEND YOU A COMMISSION CHECK FOR ALL THE INITIAL SALES WE MAKE FOR YOU! Plus, we put you in the powerful position to get paid MASSIVE SUMS OF MONEY from the revolutionary health products and unique BUSINESS that we have developed for people who care deeply about their health and want to make more money.

WHY I firmly believe our Advertising and Management Service is the perfect way HANDS-FREE WAY for you to stay home and let us make money for you:

REASON #1:

You have the leverage of up to 5 to 9 other people in your group making money for you! Leverage is THE GREATEST SECRET of the rich… and now YOU will have this power making money for you! This one reason alone could be worth a fortune to you!

REASON #2:

The best-of-the-best of the secrets and rare sources and contacts we have used to bring in over $100-Million dollars in our first 19 years alone will be making money for YOU! Yes, we have generated a HUGE FORTUNE from all of the proven secrets that we'll be using to do our best to see that YOU are getting paid the largest sum of money!

REASON #3:

We will do all of the advertising, marketing, selling, customer support, and management work for you and the other people in your group.

REASON #4:

This puts you in the powerful position to fill the hidden gap that we have discovered in the multi-billion dollar network marketing industry in a whole new, but totally proven way! And my multi-million dollar company takes care of everything for you!

But not only do we do everything for you…

We also take it ONE STEP farther than that...

REASON #5:

I will spend a significant amount of my own money to do my best to MAKE SURE you get paid the LARGEST sum of money!

Yes, you read that right…

In most cases, I will spend a significant portion of my own money to do all we can to see to it that YOU get paid the largest sum of money!

It's amazing — BUT TRUE!

Here Are The 4 Steps We Do For You Every Single Day — That Are Designed To Pay YOU The Largest Sum of Money!

STEP #1:

We will do all of the advertising for you EACH WEEK to make the largest number of sales to the people who respond to the advertising that we purchase for you.

STEP #2:

We RUSH you a weekly check for YOUR SHARE of all of the money for all the sales our experts close for you!

STEP #3:

We spend our own time, money, and expertise to do all of the follow-up marketing to all the people who did not get involved the first time. We'll stay in close touch with them, do our best to SIGN THEM UP, and add your share of the money to your next weekly commission check.

STEP #4:

A percentage of all of the people who sign up will be YOUR CUSTOMERS FOR LIFE!!! Yes, these will be YOUR CUSTOMERS and you will get paid on ALL of their monthly purchases... for life!

These 4 Steps give you the most powerful and complete money-making System ever developed! This lets us do everything for you and then pays you a generous commission for all of the sales we make for you... And that sets you up to...

GET PAID MASSIVE SUMS OF AUTOMATIC MONEY... FOR LIFE!

Yes, this is the most amazing way to let our company spend our time, work, expertise, and money to do all we can to see that YOU GET PAID the LARGEST amount of money each week and each month!

In a minute, I'll tell you how to get ALL THE DETAILS about this powerful money-making service.

But for now, let me GO BACK and tell you more about how...

Our Advertising and Management Service gives you these main benefits that you'd get in a high-dollar franchise:

1. You'll be cashing-in with products and services that are highly in demand and making other people huge sums of money with right now.

2. We give you the insider secrets that have brought us many millions of dollars.

3. We do ALL of the advertising and management for you. This includes the fact that we spend our own money on all of the complicated and expensive follow-up marketing that is absolutely

essential to making the largest number of sales.

We are not a franchise and, yet, these are the same MAJOR BENEFITS that you'll get when you get involved in a high-dollar franchise.

So please go over these main benefits.

As you'll see, this is a complete money-making service that has the powerful potential to let you sit back and make money every month — without lifting a single finger.

1. You'll be cashing-in from the millions of people who CARE DEEPLY about their health. These people are searching for products and services that can help them live longer, feel better, have more energy and vitality, and avoid the deadly diseases that are killing so many others...

The health supplement industry is booming! Tens of millions of people are constantly searching for the very best products and services that can help them live a healthier life. **These people are spending BILLIONS OF DOLLARS A YEAR on a wide variety of products and services that can help them be healthier.** And this market is growing by leaps and bounds!

More than ever before, people are OPEN and RECEPTIVE to doing all they can to become as healthy as they can be... They are spending HUGE SUMS OF MONEY on a variety of products and services that can help them live longer and feel better... They want more energy and vitality... They are terribly afraid of all of the deadly diseases that are killing their friends and loved ones before their time... And they want to make sure that they do not die from these terrible diseases...

My company is constantly searching for the very best health products and services that millions of people are searching for right now. We're always on the lookout for the little-known health products that the huge market of tens of millions of people have NOT heard about, yet. We will continue to track these items down and develop the powerful sales materials and methods that sell them for you.

Yes, when you get involved in our Advertising and Management Service, we will do all of the selling and marketing for you. We track down the very best health products that the huge market of tens of millions of people are searching for... We develop all of the advertising and marketing materials.. and we go to work to promote these products and services for you and then send you an ongoing commission check for your share of the sales.

All of this is proven in every way. Right now, as you're reading these words, there are tens of millions of people who are searching for the ultimate products and services that will help them become healthier and live longer…

This GIANT MARKETPLACE of people are spending billions of dollars a year and they are constantly searching for something that is new and different. We track these little-known health products and services down for you and then run constant advertising and marketing promotions for you that let you cash in with them… **Best of all…**

WE DO EVERYTHING FOR YOU while you sit back and collect the commission checks!

Nothing is simpler and easier…

And nothing is more proven!

How proven is this? Read on…

2. **We give you all of the insider secrets that have brought our company many millions of dollars.**

As you know, my wife, Eileen, and I began our Direct-Response Marketing company in September of 1988 with only $300.00. We used that money to buy a small ad in two magazines.

Those tiny ads were an instant hit!

We got lucky and made a profit right out of the gate… And then we used the profits from those two ads to buy two more... and then we kept expanding and rolling our profits into more and more tiny ads… Within just six months, we were bringing in an average of $16,000.00 a month and were on top of the world!

Then we got VERY LUCKY AGAIN and met marketing expert Russ von Hoelscher.

And within just 9 months, Russ helped us go from $16,000.00 a month to bringing in a grand total of almost $100,000.00 a week!

I already told you a much more detailed version of our story. And remember, I'm not trying to brag on our success or show off... I hate it when people do this and I know that YOU feel the same way. But I am bragging on the awesome power of Direct-Response Marketing and the ability to get the help, support, and guidance of the right experts who know how to make a lot of money. Russ von Hoelscher was that expert for us. **And we want to be that expert for you.**

We have been involved in this style of marketing since the late 1980s and have ran many thousands of different marketing promotions. Thanks to the success of these promotions, we have generated many tens of millions of dollars and we've learned so much. **Now we will take the best-of-the-best of everything we've learned over the years and give it to you!** And because we are your 'Joint Venture Business Partners' — we have THE STRONGEST REASON to do all we can to see to it that you get paid the largest amount of money... For more on that, read on...

3. **Because we are your 'Joint Venture Business Partner' we are happy to do ALL of the advertising and management for you, including the complicated and expensive follow-up marketing that must be done to make the largest number of sales.**

So many people 'claim' that they want to help you make money. And yet, how many of them are ready, willing, and able to spend their own money in an attempt to make sure that you get paid the largest amount of money?

The answer: very few, if any...

And yet, this is EXACTLY what we will do for you.

When you become a Client of our advertising and management service, we will take care of all of your advertising and marketing for you.

We'll run a new marketing promotion for you each week. The goal of each promotion; to reach the huge market of tens of millions of people who want to be healthier and introduce them to our health products and services.

Our goal is to get thousands of customers for our health products and services and assign these customers to our Clients like you!

As you'll see, this has the powerful potential to pay you month after month!

The reason is simple: Once people discover health products that they believe in and fall in love with, they never stop taking them!

And when these people are your customers, you will continue getting paid month after month, for as long as they continue re-ordering and using these items!

This can provide a steady income for you that continues to GROW BIGGER and never stops!

And our company has the STRONGEST REASON to do all we can to see to it that you get paid the largest amount of money for the longest period of time. The reason is simple: **We are your 'Joint Venture Business Partners.'** And because of that fact, the more money we can make for you, the more money we also make for ourselves.

That's why we are happy to do everything for you, including the powerful fact that we spend all of our own money on all of the complicated and expensive follow up marketing that must be done to generate the largest number of sales.

Good follow up marketing is the key to making the largest sum of money. This kind of marketing can be very expensive and quite complicated and, yet, the individuals and companies who do the very best job with their follow-up marketing make the largest amount of money. Now, you will be one of these people!

Best of all, you'll be sitting back and letting us do it all for you...

Our style of marketing (Direct-Response) is such an exciting way to make money.

On the surface it seems very simple and it can be. And yet, it can also be quite complicated at times and very expensive. In order to make the largest sum of money, you must know what you're doing. We do. My wife, Eileen, and I fell in love with this type of marketing back in 1988 and have been OBSESSED with learning all of the advanced methods for making the most money. **We have ran many thousands of advertising and marketing promotions for ourselves and our Clients that have generated many tens of millions of dollars...**

And now we will be running these same promotions for you on a regular basis.

This lets you sit back and make money for letting us do all of the work for you!

Does that sound too good to be true?

Maybe. And yet, it is true...

I don't blame you for being somewhat skeptical about this. After all, if you're like most people, you have worked hard all your life for the money you've earned. And now you have a company that is promising to do everything for you while you sit back and collect the commission checks for all of the sales that are made for you.

This is not too good to be true... in fact, **letting other people take care of all of the complicated, expensive and difficult work for you is...**

The secret of the world's richest people.

Yes, think about this and you'll know it's true... The world's richest people are able to sit back and let others do everything for them... These people have an army of experts who specialize in certain aspects of making money that have taken them years to master...

The world's richest people hire these experts and then sit back and let them take care of all of this difficult and complicated work. **This is one of the main reasons why the richest people continue getting even richer...** It's the fact that they hire the right experts who take care of all of the most complicated and specialized aspects of making money for them...

The average person only makes money from their own efforts, but the wealthiest people hire as many other experts as they possibly can to make money for them... And now you'll be doing this, too! In fact, thanks to modern technology, it's easier for the average person to hire experts to take care of everything for them than ever before... Specialized services are springing up everywhere... It's called 'outsourcing' and it's a BOOMING MARKETPLACE that is growing by leaps and bounds...

And now YOU will cash-in from this huge trend.

As you may know, there are all kinds of services that will take care of different aspects of advertising and marketing for you:

- They'll write and design your ads for you…

- They'll run your ads in newspapers or magazines.

- They'll write, design, and print your Direct Mail sales letters and other sales materials for you.

- They'll design and build websites for you and put them on the Internet.

- They'll take care of all the headaches and hassles of media and list selection. This helps you pinpoint the EXACT TYPE of person who is most likely to become your best long-term customer.

- They'll take care of all of your incoming calls.

- They'll do all of your data entry and manage your customer list for you.

- They'll ship out all the products for you and provide all of the ongoing services.

- They'll stay in close touch with your prospective buyers… answer all objections… and do all they can to make the initial sale to these people.

- They'll take care of all of your customer service work, to make sure your customers are happy and continue doing more business with you.

You can find many companies who will provide EACH ONE of these necessary services for you while you sit back and let them do what they do best. **And yet, when you become a Client of our advertising and management service…**

WE PROVIDE ALL OF THESE SERVICES TO YOU… UNDER ONE ROOF!

Yes, we take care of all aspects of the advertising and marketing for you. **Everything from lead generation to customer service.**

It's all done under one roof!

You'll be sitting back… every week… letting us take care of all of the most complicated and specialized forms of marketing that we have been doing since 1988. Yes, you'll be making money by letting us do the same type of advertising and marketing for you that we have been doing for ourselves, since the late 1980s…

Over the years, we have perfected our marketing methods.

We're constantly testing new methods and taking the things that work the VERY BEST and adding it to our marketing methods. In other words, **whenever we discover newer and better ways to make more money, we will be adding it to the regular marketing promotions that we do for you!** This lets you sit back and let us do our very best to make sure that you get paid the largest sum of money for the longest period of time.

And now, for a limited time when you become Client for our top level Advertising and Management Service…

We will RUSH you our valuable 'Alkaline Water Ionizer' for free! This amazing machine is designed to help you SOLVE the two major problems that cause aging and deadly disease… it's a full $947.50 value, yours absolutely free!

According to a medical doctor that I'll introduce to you in a minute, **"The TWO MAIN CAUSES of all aging and disease are low pH and free radicals."**

According to many Medical Doctors and other health professionals **Antioxidant Alkaline Water that is created by using a water ionizer solves these two problems.** Ionized water is simply passed through a water ionizer to take our impurities and ACIDIC IONS before delivering it to your glass.

In a minute, I will go into more details about the power of Alkaline Antioxidant Water and tell you some SHOCKING NEWS that concerns your health. But first, **let me introduce the medical doctor who said that alkaline antioxidant water solves two of the major problems that cause aging and disease.**

His name is Ben Johnson, M.D..

For many years Dr. Johnson had a general medical practice where he performed surgeries, delivered babies, and much more.

In 1996, Dr. Johnson had a spinal cord injury and became disabled. He was not able to perform many of the tasks of his practice. So when a long time friend suggested that he help with a chelation clinic, he agreed.

He became fascinated with alternative medicine from all the questions he was asked by his patients. He began to learn that...

There were entire fields of medicine that no one had ever told him about.

Because of all of this, Dr. Johnson decided to get a formal education in natural medicine. He went back to school and received his naturopathic medical degree and he has been practicing alternative medicine for a number of years and was a partner in an alternative cancer clinic.

As an alternative medical doctor and especially treating cancer, the most important psychological issue was emotions, **but the most important physical issue was pH.** In 1931, Otto Warberg received the Nobel Prize in Medicine for discovering that a low oxygen environment in the tissues was the cause of cancer.

The cause for low oxygen level in tissue is acid pH.

Dr. Johnson has worked for years trying to develop herbs and nutrition supplements to help overcome cancer.

His biggest problem was getting the body's pH to an alkaline level.

He would try every method under the sun, but it was hard to shift their pH.

He knew that if he were able to shift their pH by providing oxygen to the cancer cells, it would have a good chance of healing them.

According to Dr. Johnson, many people do not realize that their cancer cells can be converted back to their original functions.

When he first learned about alkaline water, he became very excited!

Dr. Johnson knew that since the body was made up of almost 70% water, changing the alkalinity of that water would be a huge accomplishment. **Once the body's water pH is changed, it affects the blood's pH.** With blood being more alkaline, the oxygen can be transported better by the cells to the tissues of the body.

When Dr. Johnson learned that the alkaline water also had a tremendous oxidation reduction potential (ORP) he became even more excited. **As a medical doctor, he knew that we need antioxidants to overcome free radical damage to our skin, liver, brain, tissues, and basically everywhere in our body.**

The alkaline antioxidant water solves the two major problems that cause aging and disease; low pH and free radicals. **It helps you get healthy and stay healthy by the alkalization of the blood and the antioxidant potential or the oxidation reduction potential (O.R.P.).**

According to Dr. Johnson, alkaline anti oxidant water is probably the most profound discovery of our time.

Dr. Johnson states: "Solutions are usually exquisitely simple. **We are looking for them in all the wrong places when choosing medicine from drug companies."**

He continues: **"Alkaline antioxidant water changes everything physiologically.** It allows the enzyme systems to work the way they should. The alkalinity allows oxygen to get to tissues. More importantly, it provides ready antioxidants to keep our bodies from rotting and rusting through the process of oxidation. Dr. Johnson is often asked: "Who should be drinking the alkaline antioxidant water?"

His answer is simple: "everyone from children to octogenarians." (octogenarians is a person between 80 and 89 years old. I had to look that one up!)

Now let me give you the words of another Medical authority: Dr. Casey Carter.

Here's what Dr. Carter has to say about the amazing health benefits of Alkaline Water:

"Alkaline antioxidant water helps get living water into your body so that you can live with better health. The ionization causes the water molecules to be just the right size to get into your cells. It's sort of like having the right key to fit a lock. Regular water has molecules that are too big to get into the cells.

Drinking regular water and expecting it to get into your cells and hydrate you is like throwing softballs at a chain linked fence and expecting them to get through to the other side. They are too big. Drinking alkaline antioxidant water is like throwing marbles through a chain link fence.

There are three essential properties to alkaline antioxidant water that are necessary for the water to work as phenomenally as it does. **These three properties are negative ORP, micro-clustering of water molecules, and an alkaline pH.**

Negative ORP.

Negative oxidation reduction potential is the gaining of electrons which have a negative charge. **Any time you are gaining electrons you are gaining a negative charge which is positive for your health.** In this unique case, negative equals positive benefits. You are anti-oxidizing. Any time you are losing electrons, you are gaining a positive charge which is negative for your health.

For instance, soda is one of the highest oxidants that you can put into your body. You do not want oxidants in your body if you want to live disease-free. Negative ORP is the anti-oxidant and anti-inflammatory component of the ionized alkaline antioxidant water.

Micro-Clustering of Water Molecules.

Water needs a way to get into the cells. If water has big molecules it can not get into the cells and hydrate the cells. That is why you can drink gallons of tap or bottled water and still be dehydrated.

Imagine that all cells have little entry gates and that molecules have to be just the right size to get through the gates. The analogy that I like to use is that if you lock elbows with 5 or 6 friends and try to get through a gate you can make it through. However, if you lock elbows with 30 friends, you cannot get through

The ideal size for molecules to get into the cells is 5 or 6 clustered molecules. This is key. This is a precise, peer-reviewed and researched science and by no means a guessing game. The Japanese have known this for decades and it's only recently beginning to be studied and understood by scientists in the West.

Our acidic environment is the perfect environment for disease to manifest. Water at the proper molecular structure does not support disease and death. **It promotes health and life.** Alkaline antioxidant water, which is at a molecular structure of 5 to 6 clusters, is perfect for our health because it can hydrate the cells.

Alkaline pH.

It is important to change the pH of the water to achieve a high alkaline level. **We are mostly water and drinking alkaline antioxidant water is the fastest way to positively impact health eradicate inflammation and disease.**

It's important to note that establishing an alkaline metabolism and alkaline blood pH are not the same thing. Alkaline antioxidant water will alkalize your metabolism, but not through your blood pH. Toxins from your environment, stress, diet, and many others cause your metabolism pH to become acidic and unbalanced. Your blood pH will always be between 7.34 to 7.44. **Alkaline antioxidant water helps balance your metabolism which directly influences the maintenance of your blood pH.** Alkaline antioxidant water and the three main components, including negative ORP, micro-clustering of water molecules, and alkaline pH all must work together for the water to enhance your optimal health. All cells need to be able to effectively take in water molecules in order to survive.

The micro-clustering of the water is what allows the water to enter the cells and give the body what every cell in the body needs to survive. If the cells do not get the essentials, they begin to oxidize and mutate. When cells mutate, problems such as cancer and many other horrible diseases are created.

Every disease has an inflammatory component. Alkaline antioxidant water is not a panacea, but drinking it affects every system of the body by affecting inflammation. **Alkaline antioxidant water alkalizes and reduces inflammation in each cell.** Everybody should set a goal to drink two thirds of their body weight of Alkaline antioxidant water in fluid ounces per day.

Alkaline antioxidant water is the single most exciting product that I have ever seen hit the health and wellness industry in my 30 year career. Water is the foundation for life and should be at the bottom of the food chain diagram.

People are needlessly suffering and dying because of unhealthy water. Alkaline antioxidant water is lifesaving. The leading causes of non-accidental death are cancer, heart attack, stroke and improperly prescribed

NOTES

211

medications.

It is so vital to remember that 50 percent of all medications prescribed are anti-inflammatory medications. People are suffering and dying needlessly because they are relying on anti-inflammatory drugs to cure them when all they need to do is drink alkaline antioxidant water. **As a doctor, my advice to everyone is to just drink the water.** It can only do you good."

So please consider the comments from these two medical authorities.

And then consider this:

Now you can drink all of the extremely healthy Alkaline Antioxidant Water you want... for free!

Yes, no cost whatsoever!

Because when you join our top level Advertising and Management Service, you will receive our 'Alkaline Water Ionizer' absolutely free!

This is a $947.50 value — yours at NO COST!

Why are we giving away our $947.50 'Alkaline Water Ionizer' absolutely free?

That's simple, but amazingly powerful. You see, we know that you are very serious about your health or you wouldn't be reading this book right now. And if you've read carefully, you know why we firmly believe that **alkalizing your body** is the most important thing you can do for your health. And many leading experts say that the very best way to do this is to drink alkaline antioxidant water.

And all you have to do is become a Client of our Advertising and Management Service at the highest level and our valuable 'Alkaline Water Ionizer' — worth $947.50 — is yours absolutely free!

This powerful water ionizer gives you all of the same health benefits that other water ionizers that sell for up to $4,000.00 or more give you.

Yes, you'll get the same healthy alkaline antioxidant water from our ionizer that you'd get with other ionizers that sell for $3,000.00 to

$4,000.00 or more.

So our 'Alkaline Water Ionizer' is a bargain at the regular price of $947.50.

But you won't pay $947.50…

You won't even pay $500.00…

Or even $50.00...

Because by joining our top-level position in the 'Advertising and Management Service — **you will get this valuable 'Alkaline Water Ionizer' absolutely free!**

But there's more! I have so much more to tell you about this valuable service and how it has the power to make you enormous sums of money!

So please send for my FREE REPORT and INVITATION that gives you all the amazing secrets... risk free!

Just give my office a call and we will RUSH you a very detailed report that tells you exactly how this powerful Advertising and Management Service can make you huge sums of money without lifting a single finger! **There's NO Obligation to get all the details.** Just call my office at **1-620-367-2600** and we'll RUSH you this complete information package by First Class Mail right away.

www.ingramcontent.com/pod-product-compliance
Lightning Source LLC
Chambersburg PA
CBHW080048280326
41934CB00014B/3251